One world,
One task

**Report of the Evangelical Alliance
Commission on World Mission**

Scripture   Union
5 Wigmore Street
London W1H OAD

Unless otherwise indicated, Biblical quotations are taken from the Revised Standard Version.

ISBN 0 85421 297 3

Printed by A. McLay & Co., Cardiff and London

Contents

Introduction

Introduction

At the National Assembly of Evangelicals, held in Church House, Westminster, in October, 1968, a Resolution was passed as follows:
This Assembly recognizes the call of God to all evangelicals to a renewal of mission to the whole world, through the proclamation of the Gospel of Jesus Christ, through participation in the work of the Holy Spirit in spiritual revival and in unity of action, and through service to human need and suffering.

Therefore this Assembly calls for the setting up of a Commission on World Mission to recommend future patterns of partnership between evangelical churches, societies, and alliances in Britain and those overseas in our common God-commissioned task: the Commission to report to a future National Assembly.

As a result, the then Secretary of the Evangelical Alliance submitted a paper to the EA Council outlining the possible aims of such a Commission. In it he referred to the frustrations of missionary societies, the problems of communicating the missionary task to the younger generation, the difficulties felt by missionary councils and missionaries in adjusting to a rapidly-changing world, the tensions created by the proper desire for national Christians to control their own affairs, and the imbalance caused by the powerful appeal which material relief needs make to the younger generation.

Such a Commission should set out the facts, evaluate them, outline a contemporary theology of mission, and suggest ways in which the Church's global responsibility for missions today should be discharged. It should consist, preferably, of men and women of the younger generation, but with enough experience to be able to evaluate the evidence in a responsible way.

The Council of the EA agreed that such a Commission should be set up, and undertook to provide the necessary support in finance and administration, thus rounding off the task which it had begun with its report on evangelism in Britain, *On the Other Side*.

As originally established, the Commission consisted of:
The Rev. A. Morgan Derham (Chairman), Mr. Pedro Arana, Mr. Iain Clayre, Mr. David Edgington, Mr. David M. Gitari, Dr. W. Lees, the Rev. Bruce Nicholls, Mr. Ernest Oliver, Mr. Nigel Sylvester, Dr. Anne Townsend and Mr. Michael Wood. All of these, except two, had served as missionaries in various parts of the world, or were overseas nationals. Miss Ruth Henshall served as secretary to the Commission throughout.

During the period of its work, as is inevitable with a body of men and women involved in the Christian world mission, a number of changes took place as follows:

Mr. Pedro Arana, Mr. Iain Clayre, the Rev. Bruce Nicholls, Dr. Anne Townsend moved away, and the following were added:

The Rev. Patrick J. Goodland, Mr. Gordon Landreth, Miss Jean Rutherford and Mr. Andrew Walls.

The Rev. Bruce Nicholls had been drawing on the resources of a group of theologians, and when he returned to India a number were added to the Commission: the Rev. Dr. Colin Brown, the Rev. John Peck, Dr. Harold Rowdon; help was also given by the Revs. Julian Charley and Philip Crowe.

The Commission began its task with one valuable asset: the Evangelical Missionary Alliance had just previously set up an enquiry into the Shortcomings of Communicating the Missionary Task (ASCOT, as it came to be known, and as it is referred to here). With the help of computer facilities and questionnaires, this enquiry analysed the whole field of present-day patterns of relationships between evangelical Christians in Britain and overseas. Mr. Ernest Oliver, Secretary of the EMA, who was responsible for it, served as a member of this Commission; all the ASCOT findings were freely put at the disposal of the Commission, and they lie behind a good deal of its findings. They are not listed here in detail, since their publication and use is a matter for the General Committee of the EMA, for whom they were prepared, but their influence on this Report is considerable, and we gladly acknowledge our debt to them.

The Commission's method of operation was to subdivide its task into separate sections—roughly indicated by the chapter headings in the Report—and to allocate each section to a sub-group of two or three people, who reported back in turn to the Commission as a whole. The Commission met for a number of sessions in London, and for two short residential sessions at Gold Hill Baptist Church, Chalfont St. Peter, Buckinghamshire, to whose officers and members they gladly acknowledge their indebtedness; in this they were following in the steps of the Commission on Evangelism which produced *On the Other Side*.

One of the aims of the Commission had been defined as 'to find out the facts'. At first, the possibility of preparing and publishing comprehensive statistics of churches and missions around the world was considered. But it soon became clear that this was not a practicable (or desirable) operation. It was impracticable because the many and varied sources of information necessary to an adequate presentation are simply not available at any one centre, and to compile it would be a mammoth task. It was undesirable in any case because we were aware of the important work going on in connection with the revision of the *World Christian Handbook*. We were in touch with the Rev. David Barrett, of Nairobi, who was deeply involved in that task, and with MARC, the computer centre in Los Angeles which was collaborating in it. We felt that since the new, and greatly improved, edition of the *World Christian Handbook* would be published in 1972, and would be much more adequate than anything we could produce, we should encourage readers to wait for the basic statistical information to appear in it. We had the benefit of some of David Barrett's research, of books like the recent *Church Growth in Latin America*, and of reports such as that compiled by Leslie Brierley of the Worldwide Evangelization Crusade, in addition to the ASCOT findings.

Nevertheless, we are very much aware of the inadequacy of our statistical information; we have had to rely a great deal on the experience of members of the Commission and personal impressions of Christian leaders in many parts of the world (we sent a questionnaire to a representative group of these). At the same time, we freely admit that such impressions can give a very inadequate picture, that the global situation is so complex and so many-sided that almost any statement made about Christianity anywhere can be faulted in points of detail, and that all our judgements suffer from inevitable limitations caused by our personal environments, experience, and outlook. (Needless to say, the same limitations will affect our critics!)

In the course of our discussions, it became obvious that the high proportion of children and young people in the world (half the population of Asia is said to be under 21) calls for special attention to be paid to work with children. But the Commission did not have the time nor the specialist skills to deal adequately with this subject. In any case, we were aware of the fact that the Scripture Union, following its International Conference at Lausanne in 1969, had set up an expert Commission to study precisely this subject. Since the Scripture Union's theological and general positions are so similar to those of this Commission, there seemed to be no point in duplicating this task, and we await with interest the publication of the Scripture Union's findings. We were the more encouraged to learn that the Chairman chosen for the Scripture Union's Commission had for a while served on the EA's Commission on Evangelism responsible for *On the Other Side*, which would seem to indicate at least a basic harmony of viewpoint, if not of methodology.

It will be obvious to the reader that what we have to say is the work of a group of Christians who hold to the 'Conservative Evangelical' understanding of the nature of the gospel and of the primacy of Biblical doctrine, and who live and work in that area. Consequently, references to missionary activity are also largely concerned with the same. This is inevitable; we were called into being by representatives of evangelical churches and movements, and commissioned to report to others of them. The fact that many areas of Christian activity and enterprise in the world today are not mentioned implies no judgment either way as to their worth or validity in the whole. We have tried to be positive without being polemical, definite without being sectarian, and Biblical without being blinkered. We also have had in mind that Christians in the traditional 'sending' countries of the Western world are more inhibited in matters of sharing and co-operation than their brothers on what used to be called 'the field'. We have therefore tried to avoid saying things which would unnecessarily embarrass worthy servants of the gospel overseas. But we are not unaware of the ways in which many missionaries are able and willing to cross denominational and 'party' barriers where they have felt this to be necessary for the sake of the gospel.

Finally, we would ask that readers of this Report should remember that the Commission was made up (as any worthwhile group concerned with World Mission must be) of men and women already deeply involved in the missionary task of the Church in one or other of its aspects. None of them had the time that they would have liked to give to this task. Much of the report has been produced under pressure, and shows it; but nevertheless we are united in presenting it with all its inadequacies, as a basis for discussion and an attempt to focus the issues confronting the people of God in the world today as they try to carry out the Lord's command to carry the gospel 'to the ends of the earth' (Acts 1.8). It is not unanimous in the sense that every member, if pressed, would underwrite every sentence of it. But it does reflect a general consensus of opinion and concern, and as such is sent out in the Name of Him who first gave both form and content to the Church's worldwide mission. The need to keep to a publishing deadline meant that most members of the Commission saw proofs only of that section in which they had been directly involved; queries which were raised at this stage could not be dealt with by the Commission as a whole, and were left to the judgment of the chairman, who took ultimate responsibility for the final version.

The placing of the chapter on 'The Theology of Mission' caused the Commission some concern. If it were placed last, it would mean that readers would have an easier introduction to the reading of the Report. On the other hand, this would make it seem something of an 'appendix', whereas it is crucial to the entire discussion. Readers may well by-pass it and plunge into Chapter 2, 'The World as it is';

but we would urge them not to avoid the work involved in working through Chapter 1 before they lay the Report down; it is fully indexed and annotated, and contains much useful study material.

Chapter 1

The Theology of Mission

1 General Outline

(*a*)   God and His World

Underlying all that the Biblical writers say about human life is the conviction that this is God's world. The thought runs through both the Old Testament[1] and the New.[2] The God who made the universe is not some unknown deity or impersonal power, but He who made Himself known in ancient Israel as Yahweh,[3] the Lord who made all things[4]. In the course of time God revealed Himself as Father, Son, and Holy Spirit. All three persons were God, and all three were active in creation[5].

From this view of the world as God's creation several things follow. (*1*) *Man is responsible to his Maker for what he says, thinks, and does.* Man is not merely an animal, driven along by unconscious urges. The Bible pays man the compliment—at times seemingly intolerable—of regarding him as an accountable person. This accountability affects not only man's 'religious' life, but his personal, social and political relationships. It is on the whole range of these relationships that the Bible speaks to man as the Word of God, addressing him as a rational person, capable of response.[6]

(*2*) *The whole of life is, therefore, God's concern.* The 'spiritual' and 'devotional' cannot be isolated from the rest of life. It is precisely in the details of man's daily life that the 'spiritual' makes itself felt. Christian witness and concern can never, therefore, restrict itself to 'religion'. Whenever we attempt to do so, we tacitly admit that our conception of God is too small.

(*3*) *The Bible speaks to man against the background of man's awareness of God.* This awareness may be dim and on occasion denied.[7] Nor is this the same as saying that man naturally responds to God. The reverse is the case. Nevertheless, man's existence as a creature in the world carries with it an awareness of God as the

11

One with whom in the end he has to do.[8] But this knowledge of God is not the sole knowledge of God.

(4) *It is through His Word that God makes Himself known, interprets man's existence, and directs his path.* It is God's Word, spoken through Jesus, the prophets and apostles, that makes possible significant, personal relationship between God and man.[9] The Christian Church must, therefore, treat with utmost seriousness what Scripture says about God and man. It is the starting point and criterion for the Church's thoughts about mission.

(b) Man's Alienation

Our TV sets, radios and newspapers forcibly remind us every day of man's alienation from his fellow man. The Bible declares that the root of all alienation is man's turning away from God, his Maker. In turning from God's ways, man turns away from his fellow man.

Man's alienation is graphically depicted in the story of Adam wanting to make himself like God and thus forfeiting his true manliness.[10] His self-seeking action brought in its train that resentment, guilt, and alienation which penetrate to the very core of man's being. The Bible pictures sin for us in various ways. It is seen as transgression of God's law and ways for man.[11] It involves guilt, making men liable to condemnation and the just deserts of their actions.[12] All men are guilty before God. Sin, and the estrangement that it brings, are not merely a matter of overt acts such as stealing, adultery, and murder. These are but some of the grosser expressions of the deep-seated corruption of human nature which no amount of concealment—even by religious acts—may eradicate.[13]

(c) Reconciliation

The Christian message proclaims that God does what man cannot do for himself. He puts away man's guilt, overcomes the enmity and brings about reconciliation. The joyful proclamation of God's grace is central not only to the New Testament but to the Old as well. For the one is a development of the other. In both the free grace of God is the only means of reconciliation.[14]

The ground of reconciliation was only progressively revealed in the Old Testament.[15] The witness of the New is that reconciliation is the work of Christ alone who poured out His blood 'for many for the remission of sins'.[16] The death of Christ is described in the New Testament in different ways: a ransom,[17] redemption,[18] propitiation,[19] the ground of reconciliation[20] and justification,[21] the means of dealing with the curse of the law, and thus also of overcoming the powers of evil.[22]

The apostle Paul pictured himself and his fellow workers as 'ambassadors for Christ, God making His appeal through us. We beseech you on behalf of Christ, be reconciled to God. For our sake He made Him to be sin who knew no sin, so that in Him we might become the righteousness of God.'[23] Reconciliation is not effective without the response of faith which turns away from sin and appropriates Christ. It is only then that justification is complete.[24] It is only thus that man receives new life in Christ.[25]

The Christian witness bears testimony not only to the forgiveness of sins but also to the new life which God gives in Christ. Sometimes the Biblical writers speak of begetting and giving birth,[26] sometimes of bringing to birth again,[27] sometimes of renewal,[28] and also of a 'new creation'[29] and a 'new man'.[30] The believer has been made alive with Christ through His resurrection.[31]

(d) The People of God

Life is a stewardship. Every man will appear before the judgment seat of Christ to give account of the use he has made of it.[32] But life is not a matter of isolated individualism. (Part of that judgment will be on how we behave with our fellow men.) God made man in His own image, and an aspect of that image is the mutual fellowship in which man was made to live.[33]

The promises of salvation which run right through scripture are concerned with the people of God as well as individuals. It could be said that the central theme of the Bible is the promise of God to His people: 'I will be your God and you shall be My people.'[34] Everything that is said in Scripture about the acts of God is an expression of this theme. The means by which this promise was realized was the covenant of grace. In it God solemnly undertook to sustain His people. On the part of the people the covenant required the response of obedience. The covenant was first made with Abraham and renewed from time to time in Israel's history.[35] Already in the Old Testament the prophet Jeremiah looked forward to a new covenant, wider in scope and greater in blessing.[36] Jesus himself declared that His death was the means of instituting the new covenant.[37] The sacrament of the Lord's Supper was its sign. Its blessings were extended to men and women of all nations, and they now specifically included the remission of sins.

The Biblical writers pictured the reconstituted people of God in various ways. Jesus himself called it His 'church'.[38] Corporately it was pictured as the bride of Christ,[39] the body of which Christ is the Head,[40] and the new Israel, the pilgrim people of God.[41]

The church is also the temple, the place where God dwells, the meeting-place of God and man in personal relationship.[42]

When a man becomes a Christian, he thus not only becomes a child of God; he becomes a member of the people of God. He lives in the world, and his responsibilities—far from being diminished—are all the greater.[43] Nevertheless, his 'commonwealth is in heaven'.[44] He looks for 'a better country—that is, a heavenly one'.[45] His concern should be first and foremost with the kingdom of God and His righteousness.[46] The basic rule of the kingdom is: 'You shall love the Lord your God with all your heart, and with all your soul, and with all your mind. This is the great and first commandment. And the second is like it, You shall love your neighbour as yourself. On these two commandments hang all the law and the prophets.'[47]

Through the covenants, Israel—and later the new Israel—were constituted as a people set apart. In both cases the people of God were not envisaged as a collection of individuals with certain common inclinations, but as a closely knit fellowship, a community, membership of which was the most important fact about a man. The new Israel has baptism and the Lord's Supper as its covenant signs. Its local expression is the assembly of believers in a given place. In the New Testament, each local church was characterized by the ministry of the Word and sacraments and a regulated church order, though details varied from place to place.[48] Membership of the visible church was very important—both to those inside and also to those outside. The New Testament recognizes no Christianity which does not take membership of the visible church seriously.

In modern times it is easy to lose sight of the fact that the Word of God was first given to the covenant community. The Law was given as the teaching by which the people of God should direct their lives.[49] It was not itself something irksome, but a means of grace, the expression of the wisdom, mind, and loving concern of God for the lives of His people. The Law was intended to point men to God. It is only when men try to use it as a means of self-justification that it becomes evil.[50] Jeremiah looked forward to the time of the new covenant when, instead of being abolished, the Law would be written on man's heart.[51] Jesus Himself endorsed the Old Testament utterance: 'Man shall not live by bread alone, but by every word that proceeds from the mouth of God.'[52] What Jesus Himself offers men is not simply life after death. He calls on them to build their lives on the rock of His teaching,[53] and to take upon themselves His yoke, so that they may be harnessed together with Him in His work.[54] But in following His teaching, men share also His life and the power of His Spirit.[55] The life He offers is one which overcomes the world.[56]

14

(e) The Last Things

However true it may be that modern men are not interested in talk of judgment, the coming judgment is a reality on which Jesus and the New Testament writers constantly dwelt.[57] A considerable part of their labours and mission was therefore devoted to pleading with men to turn to God in penitence and faith. The other side of this belief was the joyful hope with which they looked forward to a new heaven and earth and the consummation of the kingdom of God.[58]

(f) Mission and Message

When taking last leave of the elders of Ephesus, the apostle Paul reminded them that he was innocent of their blood, 'for I did not shrink from declaring to you the whole counsel of God'.[59] The same obligation rests upon the Church today. For Jesus gave the Church the commission and promise: 'Go therefore and make disciples of all nations, baptizing them in the name of the Father and of the Son and of the Holy Spirit, teaching them to observe all that I have commanded you; and lo, I am with you always, to the close of the age.'[60]

(*1*) *Mission and Response*. Mission is therefore a response of the Church to the call of Christ to proclaim the whole counsel of God. But mission itself demands a response. It summons men to repentance and faith, to fellowship in the people of God, living out the life of Christ, in the hope of the realization of the kingdom.

(*2*) *Mission and the Power of God*. Mission can only be carried out in the power of God. Here, as in all things, the Church is called to work out its salvation in fear and trembling, 'for God is at work in you, both to will and to work for His good pleasure.'[61] It is also repeatedly reminded that salvation is from first to last the gracious work of God, Who is in control of everything working out His purposes.[62]

(*3*) *Mission and Reconciliation*. The mission of the Church is a mission of reconciliation. There is a sense in which this is true, and a sense in which it is not true. In Christ men are brothers. Difference of nationality and culture pale into insignificance.[63] Self-seeking has no place in His kingdom. It is not the mission of the Church to set itself up as a kind of United Nations peace-keeping organization[64]—though such bodies have their place.

(*4*) *Mission, Service, and Message* (see further, Section III). Mission is a form of service which often involves humiliation, self-sacrifice, and concern for the material welfare of those whom the Church is sent to serve. In this the Church follows the example of her Lord.[65] But this service is not to be confused with the gospel

15

message. It is no substitute for the latter. All Christians are called to behave like the Good Samaritan.[66] But the latter parable is not the whole gospel. The Church is called to warn men of their state in the eyes of God and proclaim God's gracious salvation in Christ alone.[67]

(5) *Mission and Building up the Body of Christ.* The apostle Paul saw his travails and sufferings as completing what was 'lacking in Christ's afflictions for the sake of His body, that is the Church.'[68] Mission is concerned with building up the body of Christ. The Church has spread over every continent, but it is not like a colonial power or a vast commercial corporation with branches all over. The basic unit of the Church is the congregation of believers in a particular place. Pan-denominationalism is an un-Biblical and unhealthy concept. This is not to say that there should be no links between various churches and bodies. On the contrary. But such links should never be such that the general oversight and policy-making are in the hands of some external body. Where such bodies exist, they should serve and not rule. It also follows from the New Testament picture of the Church that patterns which have proved their use in one place are not necessarily obligatory in another. The New Testament envisages no overall uniformity of government, structures, and worship throughout the churches. It does, however, envisage fellowship and mutual co-operation between them.

(6) *The Goal of Mission.* The New Testament does not envisage the possibility of persuading all men in this life of the truth of its message. Indeed, it sees much hardship and suffering confronting the Church. But it looks also towards a final consummation when all will acknowledge the lordship of Christ and when the Kingdom is finally delivered to the Father and evil overcome and judged.[69] In this joyful expectation the Church proclaims the gospel of the Kingdom.

16

1. Gen. 1-3; Isa. 40. 25-31; 42.5; 45.18; Jer. 10.12-16; Amos 4.13; Psa. 33.6-9; 90.2; 102.25; Neh. 9.6; Job. 38.1-42. 6.

2. Matt. 6.26ff.; 10.28ff.; John 1.1ff.; Acts 17.24-31; Rom. 1.20, 25; 11.36; Eph. 3.14f.; Col. 1.16f.; Heb. 1.2; 11.3; Rev. 4.11; 10.6.

3. Ex. 3.11-15; 6.3 and throughout the Old Testament.

4. Isa. 44.24; 45.12.

5. Creation is attributed to the Father (Isa. 44.8; Mal. 1.6; 2.10; Matt. 6.8-15; Eph. 3.14f.); the Son (John 1.3; 5.17; Col. 1.16f.; Heb. 1.2;) and the Spirit of God (Gen. 1.2; Job. 26.13; Psa. 33.6; 104.29f.).

6. This holds true, whether we think of the Law in the Old Testament summed up in the Ten Commandments (Ex. 20.1-17); the pronouncements of the prophets (e.g. Isa. 1; Amos 1-3); the sermon on the Mount (Matt. 5-7); or the teaching of the New Testament epistles (e.g. Romans 12-13; 1 Pet. 2-3; and the epistle of James).

7. Psa. 14.1; 53.1.

8. Psa. 19.1ff.; Rom. 1.19f., 32; Acts 14.17; 17.22-31; The existence of God is presupposed by the Biblical writers as the common ground between them and their readers.

9. Here we might instance the prophetic 'Thus says the Lord . . .' and the dominical 'Truly I say to you . . .'; the cry of the Psalmist, 'Thy word is a lamp to my feet and a light to my path' (119.105); Jesus' endorsement of the Law and the Prophets (Matt. 5.17-19); and that of other New Testament writers (2 Tim. 3.16f.; 1 Pet. 1.24f.; 2 Pet. 1.21.).

10. Gen. 3; cf. Rom. 5.

11. Rom. 1.32; 2.12ff.; 4.15; 5.13; Jas. 2.9f.; 1 John 3.4.

12. Rom. 3.19; 5.18; 6.23; Eph. 2.3.

13. 1 Ki. 8.46; Ps. 143.2; Prov. 20.9; Isa. 6.5; Jer. 17.9; Matt. 15.18ff.; Mk. 7.1-23; Lk. 6.45; Rom. 3.12; 8.7f.; Gal. 5.17; Eph. 4.17-19.

14. The point is illustrated in Romans 4, where Paul speaks of the faith of David and Abraham. 'Blessed are those whose iniquities are forgiven, and whose sins are covered; blessed is the man against whom the Lord will not reckon his sin' (Rom. 4.7f.; cf. Ps. 32.1f.); 'Abraham believed God, and it was reckoned to him as righteousness' (Rom. 4.3; cf. Gen. 15.6; Gal. 3.6; Jas. 2.23.).

15. It was foreshadowed by the sacrificial system of the Law of Moses (cf. Heb. 10), and the Suffering Servant of Isa. 52.13ff., 53.

16. Matt. 26.28; cf. 1 Cor. 10.16; 11.25.

17. Mark. 10.45; Matt. 20.28; 1 Tim. 2.6; 1 Pet. 1.18; Rev. 5.9.

18. Eph. 1.7; Gal. 3.13; 4.5; Col. 1.14; Tit. 2.14; Heb. 9.12, 15; cf. John 8.34; Rom. 6.17,23; 7.14; 1 Cor. 1.30; 6.20; 7.22f.. Other passages speak of the completion of redemption in the end time when the work of Christ will have borne its full fruit (Lk. 21.28; Rom. 8.23; Eph. 1.14; 4.30; Rev. 14.3f.).

19. Rom. 3.25; 1 John 2.2; 4.10.

20. Rom. 5.10f.; 2 Cor. 5.18ff.; Eph. 2.11ff.; Col. 1.19ff.

21. Rom. 3.24-28; 4.24f.; Gal. 3.24; cf. 1 Cor. 1.30.

22. Gal. 3.13f.; Col. 2.13ff.

23. 2 Cor. 5.20.

24. Gal. 2.16; Rom. 3.22ff.; 5.1; Eph. 2.8; John 1.12f.

25. Col. 2.12; 3.1-3; Gal. 2.20; Rom. 8.1ff.; 2 Cor. 5.17.

26. John 1.13; 3.3-8; 1 John 2.29; 3.9; 4.7; 5.1,4,18.

27. 1 Pet. 1.3,23; John 3.3,7 speak of being born from above.

28. Rom. 12.2; 2 Cor. 4.16; Col. 3.10; Tit. 3.5.

29. 2 Cor. 5.17; Gal. 6.15.

30. Eph. 2.15; 4.24.

31. Eph. 2.5; Col. 2.13; 3.1; 1 Pet. 1.3.

32. Rom. 14.10; 2 Cor. 5.10; Matt. 25.14-46.

33. The plurality in the Godhead is projected into the creature, cf. Gen. 1.26: 'Then God said, "Let us make man in our image, after our likeness; and let them have dominion over the fish of the sea, and over the birds of the air, and over the cattle, and over all the earth, and over every creeping thing that creeps upon the earth."'

34. Ex. 6.7; Lev. 26.12; Jer. 7.23; 11.4; 30.22; 31.33; 32.38; 2 Cor. 6.16; Heb. 8.10; Rev. 21.3.

35. Gen. 15 and 17; Ex. 24 cf. also 2.24; 6.4ff. Although there is no record of the making of a covenant with David, it would seem that God made one with him (Ps. 89.3f.; 26ff.; 2 Sam. 7.12-17). The latter was ultimately messianic in its reference (Isa. 42.1,6; 49.8; 55.3f.; Mal. 3.1; Lk. 1.32f.; Acts 2.30-36). The covenant was renewed under Josiah (2 Ki.23) and Ezra and Nehemiah (Neh. 9-10).

36. Jer. 31.31ff., cf. Ezek. 36.26ff.; 37.14; Heb. 8.8-12; 10.16f.; Lk. 1.67-79.

37. Matt. 26.28; Mk. 14.24; Lk. 22.20; 1 Cor. 11.25; Heb. 10.29.

38. Greak *ecclesia* (Matt. 16.18; 18.17) means *assembly*, a word which was used for the assembly of Israel, constituted at Sinai and assembled from time to time before the Lord. The word recurs throughout the New Testament.

39. Mk. 2.19f.; Matt. 25.1ff; John 3.29; 2 Cor. 11.2; Eph. 5.25ff.,31f.; Rev. 19.7; 21.2; 22.17;. The picture is in fact an extension of an Old Testament picture of Israel which also was viewed as the bride of Yahweh (Isa. 54.6; Jer. 2.2; 3.20. Ezek. 16.8; 23.4; Hos. 2.16).

40. Rom. 12.5; 1 Cor. 10.16f.; 12.12,21,27; Eph. 1.23; 2.16; 4.4,12,16; 5.23; Col. 1.18,24; 2.19; 3.15.

41. Rom. 9-11; Gal. 3.16; Eph. 2.11-22 which combines several of these images, Jas. 1.1; 1 Pet. 1.1; 2.9-12; cf. Matt. 19.28; Lk. 22.30; John 10.16.

42. 1 Cor. 3.16f.; 2 Cor. 6.16—7.1; Eph. 2.19-22; 1 Pet. 2.4-10; Heb. 12.22f.; Rev. 3.12; 21.2ff.; cf. Mk. 14.58; 15.29; Matt. 21.42; Ps. 118.22f.; Acts 4.11.

43. Matt. 22.15-22; Rom. 13.1-10; Phil. 1.27; 2.14ff.; 1 Pet. 2.11ff.

44. Phil. 3.20.

45. Heb. 11.16.

46. Matt. 6.33.

47. Matt. 22.37-40; cf. Deut. 6.5; Lev. 19.18; Mk. 12.28-34; Lk. 10.25-28.

48. The oversight of the New Testament churches was in the hands of elders or bishops. The two names were synonymous, and there were apparently more than one in each church. See Acts 14.23; 15.6,22; 20.17, 28; Phil. 1.1; 1 Tim. 3.1-7; Tit. 1.5ff. Some churches at least had deacons (Phil. 1.1; 1 Tim. 3.8-13), though they were not mentioned by name in Acts. There were also other gifts and ministries which varied from place to place and from time to time (Rom. 12.6ff.; Eph. 4.11ff.; 1 Cor. 12.4ff.).

49. Cf. Ex. 20.1ff.; 21.1ff.; 24.3; Lev. 19.1ff.; Deut. 4.1ff.; Josh. 1.7ff.; Neh. 10.29.

50. Rom. 2-3 and Gal. 2-3 set out Paul's exposition of the function of the Law in showing what is required of man and thus of how far short he falls of God's standards, and how only Christ can atone for man. But the Law is not an arbitrary, artificial standard. It is precisely because it expresses what is justly required of man that it justly condemns him.

51. Jer. 31.33.

52. Matt. 4.4; cf. Deut. 8.3.

53. Matt. 7.24-27.

54. Matt. 11.29f.

55. Matt. 18.20; 28.18f.; John 14.15-31; Rom. 8.5ff.; Gal. 6.8.

56. John 16.33; Rom. 8.37; Rev. 3.21.

57. Matt. 3.2; 5.21ff.; 21.33-43; 22.1-14; 24.37ff.; 25.14-46; Lk. 10.13-16; 11.32; John 3.16-21; Acts 17.31; Rom. 14.10; 2 Cor. 5.10.

58. In addition to the passages already noted in connection with judgment see also Rom. 8; 1 Cor. 15; Phil. 1.23; 2.9ff.; 1 John 3.2; Rev. 21-22.

59. Acts 20.27.

60. Matt. 28.19f.; John 20.21-23.

61. Phil. 2.13.

62. Matt. 11.27; 13.11; John 1.12f.; 6.37ff., 44f.; 10.27ff.; 13.8; 15.19; 17.6,9,11f.,19ff.,24; Rom. 8.28ff.; 9.1-11.36; Eph. 1.4-12; 2.1-10; Tit. 1.1; 1 Pet. 2.4-10.

63. Eph. 2.11-16; Phil. 3.4-11.

64. Matt. 10.21,35; 12.30.

65. Mk. 10.43ff.; John 13.1-16; Phil. 2.5-11.

66. Lk. 10.29-37.

67. John 14.6; Acts 4.12; Eph. 2.1-10.

68. Col. 1.24.

69. Matt. 25.31-36; 1 Cor. 15.25-28; Phil. 2.11; Eph. 1.9f.; Rev. 21.1-5.

2 Regeneration and Conversion

Our Lord speaks of regeneration as 'being born of the Spirit'.[1]

When the Bible talks about the Spirit of God, it refers to God at work, with effects that anyone present would actually experience for himself and be able to talk about afterwards. Indeed, in the case of the prophets and early Christians, they could not help talking about it![2]

Nowadays the concept of 'the Spirit' is commonly a very vague one, but for the men of the Scriptures it was not: He was the Spirit of Israel's God, and in the New Testament the Spirit of the Lord Jesus Christ, having His clearly defined character. So when Jesus spoke of being born of the Spirit, He was referring to a change in a person's life which that person would experience and be able to talk about. It might be dramatic and obvious, or quiet and imperceptible, even hardly recognized, but nonetheless a change capable of being identified and to some extent described. In speaking of it as a birth, He identifies it as a beginning; so our concept must allow for growth, learning, improvement. It is by definition decisive, but it can at the same time go with shortcomings in knowledge, appetite for truth, clear sight, and so on.[3]

It is possible to talk about this new life in two ways. The newborn Christian often finds God so real to him that he feels his whole environment has changed: it has a new meaning, a new unity. Such a person understands himself as 'transferred into the kingdom of His beloved Son.'[4] But he may be aware of the event in a different way, as something happening inside of him. God is near, it is true, but what is so astonishing is the way this matters, with this new 'instinct' to talk to God as 'Father'.[5] Some remarkable kind of kinship has been created, such as a boy might have with his parents, sharing the same genetic stock. And he belongs to other Christians, not simply because they accept him, but because of a family kinship.[6] So, as Christians, we begin to behave differently because something in our nature has changed. We see our past life, and the life of the unregenerate, with different eyes. Our conscience begins to act differently; in some ways more strictly, and yet having a greater sense of freedom, a confidence that our failures no longer have the last word. Where fear of evil spirits has held sway, their power is broken.

One important feature of all this is that it is not only among followers of other religions that the gospel gets its converts; it claims them equally from devotees of Christianity as well! And such converts often see their past life, even at its most religious, as spiritually worthless, even sometimes a hindrance.[7] It is doubtful whether any other religionist, even a Buddhist, would write down his past devotedness so drastically. But the Scriptures speak of the Gospel as introducing a new order of things; as new, in its own way, as the Creation itself.[8]

Jesus made possible through His death an approach to God which, because it is unique and perfect, makes any other way, even that of the Old Covenant, out of date.

The great variety of human experience makes it difficult to generalize when we begin to talk about what actually happens in a person's inner experience in regeneration. Certainly, it involves all of a person there is. We might usefully refer to a conventional manner of classifying life—as 'knowing (i.e. being aware of things) leading to feeling (i.e. the experience of being impelled) leading to an act of will (i.e. in choice, decision, and action)' It is, of course, an oversimplification, but it will serve to begin.

(a)   The Place of Knowledge

How much does one need to *know* to be born again? Undoubtedly something: a 'mustard-seed' minimum.[9] Of course knowing Christ personally is more than knowing facts about Him, but the first involves the second. At least it is known 'that He is . . .'[10] The New Testament message is more than that; it is that He is 'Lord'.[11] Strangely, there are few clear references to Him as God.[12] The word 'God' has different connotations for different peoples, and is too dependent on reflection and definition. To say 'Jesus is God' is a statement of conviction at best; to say 'Jesus is Lord' is a declaration of allegiance. 'Lord', is also the Old Testament title for the God of Israel, and for the promised Christ.[13] It is moreover a personal title, implying that there is a Person with depths of character yet to be discovered. So to know Jesus as Lord is like holding a thread which leads a man to the heart of the complex maze of truth as it is in Him. The Scriptures define the truth even more precisely. He is a historical Person who died, yet lives more alive than ever.[14] The lordship is absolute, such as only God exercises, and faith must confess that salvation can owe nothing to any effort or method of man's at all. (This last fact ultimately leads to the Biblical idea of Christ's death as substitutionary.[15])

When we apply the title 'Lord' to Jesus Christ, we are using as comprehensive a term as we can to convey the essence of the impact of His personality upon us. But an individual convert may misunderstand this term if his upbringing has not given him a Biblical meaning for the word, and he might need quite different words to convey the same idea. For many religious Victorians 'our Lord' suggested no more than a call for formal acknowledgement (like 'Your Majesty'); and often the title 'Saviour' better conveyed the Biblical idea which was really needed. A missionary in Japan recalls the case of a childless widow converted on hearing Mark 3.35, by trusting Jesus as her 'son'! She lived in a society where, in the absence of a husband, the eldest son exercised complete sway over mother and household. Accordingly, the reality of Christ's Lordship is conveyed, not only by word, but by the personal impact of the bearer of the message. Even where the message is spoken, this is normally only done effectively insofar as there has been a prior personal relationship established whereby the witness has become as fully as possible identified with the recipient, especially in respect of his interests and culture (so Paul's example, 1 Cor. 9.19ff). This is not, of course, to deny the value of literature or radio. But even there the principle operates covertly in the areas of translation, attractive presentation, use of metaphorical language, not to mention intercessory prayer.

(b) Feeling and Will

It is most difficult of all to speak of the *feelings* attendant upon new birth. Some people's feelings seem to be constitutionally more dramatic than others'. In some societies their expression may be conventionally suppressed, though under the Spirit's conviction this may not hold good. Emotional energy may also be diverted to some substitute action, and feelings may even be fostered as themselves a substitute for action and decision. So the emotions are only significant insofar as they serve to engage a person's will in a total self-commitment to the Lord Jesus Christ, and generally speaking only time will reveal how far this is authentic.

The activity of the *will* can be considered under two aspects: repentance, and faith. The two Greek words in the New Testament for 'repent' refer respectively to a change of attitude (regularly associated with feelings of regret and shame), and a change of life, the two being inseparable in fact. This varies according to the extent to which the old life differs in form from the new; and to the kind of instruction received beforehand. In matters of behaviour which might be inferred from Scripture there appear to be *spiritual priorities* differing for each individual. Note also that response must be related to cultural environment. It is a dubious rule which insists that in a polygamous society a man should put away, say, three of his four wives and thereby reduce them to a defenceless destitution. Such situations are not theoretical. Some distinction

22

needs to be made between polygamy and adultery.[16] In general we can say that repentance involves a renunciation of, and a desire to discontinue, practices which the convert knows to be displeasing to God as seen in Christ.

(c) Confession of Faith

A vexed question here is that of open confession. The New Testament regards this as an essential accompaniment of the new life,[17] but this needs careful consideration. It cannot usurp the place of faith: it is a normal by-product which is an evidence of genuineness (cf. 2 Cor. 4.13). The New Testament conception of confession highlights this with its overtones of public worship, especially in connection with baptism[18], of giving account of oneself as a believer, almost always thought of in response to questioning[19], and of taking sides when challenged. But, significantly, there are no explicit commands given in the Epistles to ordinary believers to take the initiative. Col. 4.5 speaks of taking opportunities, and they could be scarce in an 'evil age' (cf. Eph. 5.16).

Baptism is, among other things, a special form of confession. It dramatically symbolizes salvation. Unlike saving faith, which can occur in the heart under any circumstances, it must wait for its occasion—available water, tests of genuineness, permission of parents for minors, and the like. It follows that not to be baptized cannot necessarily equal a denial of Christ, though it could mean that in certain circumstances. Could there, then, be circumstances when it would be right to postpone baptism of a true convert? If so, on what principles?

Baptism is the convert's normal mode of entry into the visible church (1 Cor. 12.13f, cp. the practice in Acts). For very many peoples of the earth this can only mean repudiation of one's native community for another, alien (possibly Western) one; and to do this as a private individual is a defiance of the established order of things. To condone it is to condone lawlessness. The distinction which we take for granted, that between two legitimate authorities, civil and religious (cf. Rom. 13.1ff), is inconceivable to such. Unless baptism can be understood by both participants and witnesses to declare a spiritual and not a societal allegiance, it can hardly be said to be a true 'confession'. It must be admitted that Christian teaching has sometimes disrupted local structures disastrously without replacing them with anything adequate. On the other hand, converts who have been made to wait for baptism on such grounds have sometimes been the keenest evangelists.[20] To wait for a community understanding in this does not mean wholesale compromise. Christians will stand over against their communities both by what they do, and by what they do not do.

Regeneration certainly involves membership of the Church. What relation should this bear to the convert's position in the family, caste, clan, nation? The tension already noted between two legitimate orders appears again. The family, for instance, is ordained by God in Creation, and its relationships are therefore binding. Yet its functioning is affected by the Fall; therefore it needs, and must be subject to, the work of redemption. So the convert must honour his parents, and yet be prepared to renounce them.[21] The Church cannot be a rival or substitute for family ties, and it may be part of a disciple's cross to be deprived of their comfort. But it may act as an alternative in some respects. For example, in the matter of 'identity'. Identity is largely experienced in the sense of belonging to others, and loss of it is a serious factor in undermining moral personality. Sometimes a convert is so completely extruded from the family or tribal group as to feel that he is no longer an identifiable person. The least that Christian fellowship can do is to manifest to him his new and eternal identity in the Kingdom of God.

(d) The Convert and the Community

A related question which arises in the close solidarity of many 'face-to-face' communities is that of personality dependence. Western thought is frequently too individualistic to understand this, and finds some Biblical thinking barely intelligible.[22]

A correspondent from Ceylon wrote, "I feel sure the Asian will see it (the gospel) more in community, the salvation of the people of God in a body, than we have yet seen.' In some societies, adults depend greatly on the group in making decisions. (The best known examples of this are the 'long-hut' societies of Borneo, where whole extended families live under one roof, in one room.) Many missionaries are feeling that it is wrong to aim at isolated professions of faith from those whom the group would regard as we regard younger children. The policy has, in some areas of Africa and Indonesia, for instance, borne fruit.[23] This corresponds with the Biblical conception of man as a communal being. In Scripture, people are not simply isolated units, even spiritually.[24]

The phenomenon may be highlighted by the following question: Consider two people confronted with the gospel—a young man from a family of New York socialites; another one of a 'long-hut' family. Are the causes of their hesitation comparable? Surely not. The New Yorker would know he should make a decision, but fears the cost. The 'long-hut' man holds back because he would feel it morally wrong to make his own decision. The situations are radically different. All this has led to some serious rethinking about missionary strategy, noting in particular: (i) There is a Christian obligation to go first with the gospel to those who are most free to make proper moral decisions about it, at least when it comes to open commitment. (ii) Mass-movements, however they may take place,[25] are not to be regarded with prejudiced suspicion, but as God-given opportunities. (iii) There is a vital task of Christianizing whole societies, so that a young church may grow within a community as a truly indigenous fellowship, rather than by repudiation of its culture and an artificial westernization. (iv) The relationship between what a person does when he embraces Christianity as a religion, and what happens in regeneration, needs to be thought out with a greater clarity if we are not to repeat past mistakes of confusing the new birth with membership of some Christianized social grouping, particularly in the second generation.[26] (v) The possibility that people in the 'hard' fields might be better reached through the Christianizing of 'softer' affiliated peoples.

The fact stands that God has spread His Word widely where the principle of group solidarity obtains in mass-movements; not only individuals, but whole societies have been, and are being, claimed for Him.[27] There is no evidence of a higher proportion of false conversions in these than in 'one-by-one' evangelism; the results are often remarkably stable. We are brought again to the essence of the matter, that it is not a question of the means or the circumstances whereby regeneration takes place, but of the reality of the Saviour with Whom faith deals, and His claim of absolute dominion over life and soul.

(e) Universalism

This particular discussion would not be complete without some reference to contemporary universalism. Two kinds of universalism have gained currency in the church in modern times. There is the old, 'liberal' form which maintained that since God is perfect love, He could never reject for ever any of His creatures. But there is also the quasi-universalism which finds expression in the later volumes of Karl Barth's *Church Dogmatics* which gives a universalistic interpretation to Biblical covenant theology.[28] Barth sees a union between God and man in virtue of the union between the humanity and deity in the Person of the incarnate Christ. Barth calls this the *covenant*. Because of this union God will never reject man. In dying Jesus Christ took upon Himself the curse of divine wrath.

25

Because He has borne it upon the cross, man will never have to taste that dereliction that Christ tasted. Because Christ is God's chosen One, mankind is chosen in Him. The gospel message for Barth is therefore a summons to mankind to realize that man is God's chosen partner in Christ, that man is in a real sense already in Christ, that God's wrath is a thing of the past. Man is already saved. What he needs is to realize it. Even if man rejects the Gospel, the most he can do is to try to live the life of the rejected.

Both these forms of universalism soften what seem to be the harsher features of the traditional understanding of the Christian message. But it must be said that neither can be accepted if we desire to remain faithful to the witness of the Scriptures. Furthermore, there is a sense in which both these theologies do violence to the integrity of the human personality by denying it the right and the ability to stand by its decisions and actions. Both involve a re-conciliation without a necessary change of heart and will on the part of the individual person.

There is nothing in Scripture which entitles us to understand God's love as cancelling out His holiness and justice. It is precisely the character of God in His love and holiness which leads to the cross as the way of salvation. The Bible never minimizes the seriousness of judgment.[29] Jesus no less than the writers of the epistles spoke with the utmost solemnity of the finality of judgment. Those who turn in repentance and faith are justified and reconciled.[30] The simple but genuine faith and penitence of a dying thief,[31] a des-pairing tax-collector[32] and a prodigal who has come to the end of his tether[33] find the free and unreserved love of God. But forgiveness and new life are to be found only by those who seek. The self-satisfied and self-righteous will remain as they are. 'God is not mocked, for whatever a man sows, that he will also reap.'[34]

NOTES

1. John 3.8.
2. Num. 11.26, cf. Amos 3.8; Acts 2.4.
3. 1 Cor. 8.7; Col. 1.10; 2 Pet. 1.9.
4. John 3.5; Col. 1.13.
5. Rom. 8.15; Gal. 4.6.
6. 1 John 3.10; 5.1.
7. cf. John Wesley's conversion, and the case of Paul, Phil. 3.1-7.
8. 2 Cor. 5.17, cf. 1 Cor. 15.22.
9. Rom. 10.14ff.
10. Heb. 11.6.
11. Rom. 10.9; 1 Cor. 15.1f.
12. John 1.1; John 20.28.
13. Ps. 110.1, cf. Mark 12.35f.
14. Rom. 14.9.
15. Rom. 5.6-9.
16. For New Testament principles, see art. 'Culture and Communication' by C. H. Kraft, *Practical Anthropology*, Vol. 10 (1963), No. 4.
17. Luke 12.8; Matt. 10.32ff.; Luke 9.26.
18. Acts 22.16; Rom. 10.9-13.
19. Col. 4.6ff.; 1 Pet. 3.15, cf. 1 Pet. 3.1.
20. See 'An Example of Mass Conversion' by G. F. Vicedom, in *Practical Anthropology*, Vol. 9, No. 3, and Cragg, *Call of the Minaret*, p.346.
21. Luke 14.26; Mark 7.9ff.; 1 Cor. 7.15; Eph. 5.22—6.4.
22. i.e. The judgments upon whole nations in the Old Testament, the case of Achan's family in Josh. 7. The principle of human solidarity operates both in sin, judgment and salvation, though through man's moral choice: Rom. 5.12ff.; 1 Cor. 15.21f.
23. See *Bulletin of Church Growth* LV, No. 6, p. 21; and J. C. Wold, *God's Impatience in Liberia* (Eerdman's).
24. Rom. 14.12-15 deals with the interplay between individuality and dependence in faith; the gospel tends to develop both together in the life of the Church. But spheres of mission often appear as social groups— 'nations' in Matt. 28.19; Acts 13.46; Acts 9.35; Rom. 1.16.
25. *Bulletin of Church Growth*, May 1969, cites a remarkable case of this being precipitated by government action.
26. Vicedom, *op. cit.*, is specially interesting on this question. Baptism was sharply separated from tribe conversion.
27. See J. W. Pickett, *Mass Movements in India*, N.Y., Abingdon Press, 1933. Required reading for anyone studying this subject is D. A. McGavran, *Bridges of God*, World Dominion Press: a controversial, but highly significant book.

28. For further discussion see Colin Brown, *Karl Barth and the Christian Message*, 1967, pp.133-139.

29. Cf. Matt. 7.13-27; 16.27; 18.4ff.; 25.1-46; Luke 9.62; 10.20; 17.1ff.; John 3.16ff.; 6.39ff.; 12.48; Acts 17.31; Rom. 2.1-10; 6.23; 9.1-11.36; Eph. 5.1-10; 2 Thess. 1.5-12; Heb. 6.2; 9.27; 10.26,31; 1 Pet. 4.5; Jude 4,6,21; Rev. 6.17; 20.11-15. See further Leon Morris, *The Biblical Doctrine of Judgment*, 1960.

30. Luke 18.14; Acts 2.38; 16.31; Rom. 3.19-26; 5.1; Gal. 2.16; 3.6ff.; Eph. 2.1-22.

31. Luke 23.42f.

32. Luke 18.14.

33. Luke 15.18ff.

34. Gal. 6.7.

3 The Theology of Service

(*a*)   Service in God's World

Christian service starts with the assumption that the world in which we live is basically good because God made it and sustains it.[1] What is true of creation generally is true of man's fundamental role of ruling over and caring for the created order—the so-called 'cultural mandate'.[2] Physical life is good in itself[3] and, conversely, its loss is evil, whether in the death of man or animals.[4] God has provided food for our enjoyment.[5] He has called us into community life,[6] supremely through the institution of marriage.[7] Husbandry of natural resources is a God-given task.[8] God richly provides things for our enjoyment.[9] Thus we must start from a positive view of the material world and of human society which are, at root, good.

Of course, we must also recognize that God's world is a fallen world. The Fall has profoundly affected man's situation in God's world and man's society with other men.[10] Subduing the earth, tilling it, and keeping it have become burdensome tasks. Many specific laws have had to be given both to preserve the good things in the world (life, marriage and the family, mutual trust and inter-dependence, the Sabbath[11]) and to save the wrongdoer from the further consequences of his misdeeds at the hands of other fallen men.[12] The evil bias in man means that he needs constant warning of the damaging effects of wrongdoing, and constant encouragement through reminders of the beneficial effects of doing right, as the whole Bible testifies.[13] Because all have sinned[14], every aspect of man's enterprise is bedevilled by a distortion of God's basically good world. The Christian, therefore, claims to have been given an understanding of how God's world and human society have been set up. He has the means and the incentive for making a positive contribution to society. He also comes to society's problems with a realism born both of his own personal understanding of the effects of sin in his own experience, and of a Biblical insight into the causes and effects of sin in the world as a whole. It is to be noted that Biblical principles here are related to *all* men, and not only to the people of God. They are the 'Maker's instructions' for the proper functioning of human society and the material world. This needs to be stressed in our contemporary secular culture.

The Bible lays much stress on the need for social justice. Unjust burdens were a major complaint against Pharaoh in the days of Moses[15] and the Mosaic legal code was designed to give justice to Israelite and Gentile alike.[16] The Old Testament prophets have much to say about social justice[17] and the New Testament assumes the need for it[18] and urges it as a special duty on Christians.[19] God's world is to be a just world.

(b) God's own Example of Service

Not only is the Christian to be concerned about material things and human society because God has made and ordered them: he also is impelled by the significance of the Incarnation and the example of Christ. Jesus came and shared our human situation. He was born of humble parents[20] and in a small country under colonial oppression and exploitation.[21] And He was born to *serve*,[22] and in this respect He explicitly taught that He was being an example to His followers.[23]

Little is said about Jesus and politics, but His general attitude to the political and religious authorities appears to have been one of submission, recognizing the jurisdiction of the State but bearing in mind the higher duty to God.[24] He did take physical action in protest against an abuse in the use of the Temple.[25] His teaching to His followers was so revolutionary in its demands that it would transform society if men acted on it.[26] He preached that the kingdom of heaven was at hand,[27] but showed that His kingdom was not of this world.[28]

If Jesus' total attitude to the political powers has often been found enigmatical (and His followers, then and since, have been divided as to how to interpret His teaching on the subject), His response to human suffering was immediate and plain. From the start of His ministry we see Him dealing with sickness, mental disturbance, supply problems, and premature death.[29] He commissioned His disciples to extend this ministry themselves in His name.[30] In His teaching He emphasized the need for a compassionate attitude to all men,[31] and illustrated this supremely in the story of the Good Samaritan, which shows how in God's sight the man who demonstrates practical concern for another is of more account than the merely religious.[32]

It is to be noted that, throughout the Gospels, Jesus' ministry of practical compassion goes hand in hand with His teaching ministry, which largely dealt with spiritual values—men's attitudes to God and to one another. Preaching and service were parallel activities, and inter-related.

A final aspect of the Incarnation that deserves note is that it demonstrates the spirit of service that we all ought to have—God setting aside His glory and becoming Man and a Slave.[33]

30

(c) The Church's Rôle in Service

We have seen how Jesus taught His immediate followers that they must show a practical compassion to those in need: He also commissioned them to proclaim His message—to be His witnesses.[34] These parallel rôles of preaching and service are found from the earliest days of the Church.[35] They are natural expressions of the love of God in the heart of the believer, of the new life given him by God's Holy Spirit.[36]

The forms of practical compassion shown by the early Christians were very similar to those seen in Christ's own earthly ministry, especially in healing the sick and the lame.[35] It is interesting to note that one case of raising the dead involved Tabitha, who had been 'full of good works and acts of charity'.[37] It is clear that the early Christians enjoyed a close-knit fellowship, and it is legitimate to assume that their works of mercy were often jointly undertaken and not just individual enterprises. The Early Church, in short, was a community in which compassion for those in either spiritual or material need was constantly being demonstrated and was a living part of her witness. She was being true to the command in the Sermon on the Mount, 'Let your light so shine before men, that they may see your good works, and give glory to your Father who is in heaven.'[38]

The Holy Spirit, who inspires the Christian's service and testimony, appoints different gifts to different members of the Church, some being more concerned with the spiritual and some with the material.[39] Teaching, healing, acts of mercy, administration, all have a place alongside what are nowadays called spiritual gifts, as can be illustrated from many parts of the New Testament. The example of Stephen[40] shows that no rigid distinctions should be drawn between these different gifts, as one man may have several. But each Christian is to cultivate his own particular gifts[41] in submission to the sovereignity of the Spirit.[42] The latter part of many of the New Testament epistles show how the Christian has to work at the full development of his life in the world, including his life of service.[43] The old nature is a constant hindrance and must be continually put to death.[44]

(d) Some Forms of Christian Service

Just as healing was prominent in the ministry of Jesus and in the early witness of the apostles, so too it has played a significant part in the work of the Church throughout Christian history. In view of what has already been said about the importance of the body and Christ's specific instructions to His disciples, this is hardly surprising.

31

Healing is a complex subject, and there is not room to discuss it in detail here. It can be noted, though, that the Christian will not be unduly depressed if healing does not take place: he looks for a better future. But the contribution of Christians to the progress of medicine through the ages is impressive. Not least is this true in the realm of medical missionary work in the past 150 years, during which Christian workers have given a self-sacrificing service for humanity which is unsurpassed in human history. Christian motivation gives doctors also a personal approach to their patients' needs. This is not to deny the contributions of non-Christians, nor the failures of some Christian doctors and nurses. But it can be claimed that Christians have a striking testimony in the service of medicine.[45]

Teaching is another major realm where the Church has found an important rôle. In view of what has been said about the nature of the world and of human society as under God's ultimate laws, it is legitimate for Christians both to offer their own gifts and not to be surprised that non-believers also have a contribution based on their creatureliness. The Church should encourage all study of the true, the just, the lovely, and the good.[46] As in medicine, so in teaching, the modern Christian missionary movement has often blazed a trail which those of other faiths and of none have been pleased to follow.

Welfare and social work have been the concern of the Church from the beginning, particularly within the Christian community itself.[47] It is difficult to believe that charity was limited to Christians, however, in view of the teaching of the Sermon on the Mount. In the history of modern times, Christians have been in the forefront of work among the outcasts of society, notably in the various aspects of Victorian philanthropy. (See K. Heasman: *Evangelicals in Action* (1962), an appraisal of their social work in the Victorian era.) In the present century, Christians have found a continuing ministry in helping the casualties that still occur in a welfare state.

Welfare and relief have been undertaken by Christians on a worldwide scale. In New Testament times Paul organized relief for Christians affected by a famine in Judea.[48] It could be argued that Christian charity is to begin within the Church—'Let us show good to all men, and especially to those who are of the household of faith'[49], but the example of the Good Samaritan shows that it is not to end there. In a world that has shrunk as a result of modern communications, both information about needs in distant parts and means of sending speedy relief are available as never before, and Christians have made the relief of physical disaster anywhere in the world one of their aims.

The increasing importance of governments and complex power structures in the life of modern society and of the individual raises in acute form the question of the Christian's involvement in economic and political action. Even in the last century, when Christian service concentrated on practical philanthropy, men like Wilberforce and Shaftesbury recognized the need for concerted political effort as well, and worked for the legal abolition of slavery and the legal protection of child employees. Romans 13 is the classic reference, demonstrating that even a heathen magistrate is God's servant— how much more would a Christian one be? This whole chapter argues the need for some form of political structure.[50] The whole Bible gives the impression that order is to be preferred to anarchy.[51] The trials before the end of the age are described in 2 Thessalonians 2 (RSV) in terms of lawlessness. Godly minorities are a factor in God's judgment on particular communities, as the story of Abraham's intercession for Sodom and Gomorrah shows.[52] Joseph's governorship in Egypt[53] shows how a man of God can have profound influence on the well-being of a whole nation—and beyond. In the modern world, politics, like any other honourable profession, can be seen as one in which certain Christians are called to exercise their gifts. The world of politics, and the world of industrial and economic power structures, are as much in need of Christians with their standards of honesty, integrity, and compassion, as are the worlds of medicine and education.

(e) Dangers to avoid in Christian service

Whenever Christians address themselves to cultural and practical matters, they need to recognize that the Church itself is inevitably affected at any one time by the culture of its age and location. This is obvious even from the story of the people of God in the period of history covered in the Bible. Thus we need to be careful not to confuse temporal cultural aspects of the life and service of the Church with those aspects that are eternal and fundamental. The doctrines of grace should make us particularly wary of laying down rules which are not essential.[54] Social habits die hard, and even the apostles had to learn lessons in radical rethinking of their ingrained attitudes.[55] In the modern world, mistakes have undoubtedly been made in making western cultural norms obligatory on young converts in totally different cultures, instead of prescribing only those basic principles which are given as universal in Scripture. As the culture even in one country changes alarmingly rapidly today, there is the greater need for the right sense of what really is fundamental and eternal and what is optional and transitory. We should not deny that there are exegetical problems even here—such as the extent to which 1 Corinthians 11. 2-16 is a reflection of temporal culture regarding male and female hair and head-dress.

A second danger for the Christian dealing with questions of service is that he will expect to be able to produce ideal solutions to the problems of society. These problems are soon found, however, to be incapable of ideal solutions, and both politician and social worker have often to accept the lesser evil as the best available course. Questions of opinion also arise as to which solution is the best, even if aims and ideals are all agreed. The Church will therefore generally avoid committing itself as a Church to particular political or social policies, and Christians need to trust one another when they find themselves in opposing political or social groups or classes. The difficulty of finding solutions should not deter the individual Christian from being fully involved, and on the previous argument of this section some have a definite gift for and calling to such involvement. But the Christian must not claim as God's truth what is no more than his own opinion.[56]

The idea that the Church should know how to form the ideal society can arise from a wrong identification of the Church with the Kingdom of God. The Church expects to be a minority, often persecuted, and standing over against 'the world'.[57] Christians are to be the salt of the earth,[58] interpenetrating society and reducing decay, just as salt was used in meat in New Testament times. But their action will not of itself bring in the ideal society. God's Kingdom comes on a different plane, and God *gives* it to His children[59] in the sense that in His sovereign disposition of all created things He meets His children's material needs as well as their spiritual needs. God's Kingdom came in a sense when Christ walked this earth,[60] as the King Himself was present. But it will be consummated only at the end of the age.[61]

In the present century, Evangelicals have traditionally been shy of involvement in political and social work because of its association with the 'social gospel' of theological liberalism. As already noted, their Victorian forebears had no such inhibitions, and Christ's own words about his followers being 'in but not of' the world[62] call them to a full rôle in society. But they will act in the Name of Christ,[63] not anonymously. Convinced that it is *not* inevitable that all men will be saved, they will always associate some form of Christian proclamation with their Christian presence and believe they thus accord with the New Testament picture of the witnessing Church. Peter's first recorded miracle of healing was performed explicitly 'in the name of Jesus Christ of Nazareth'[64]. So it can be argued that the Church, including the local congregation, should be seen to be involved in social concern as part of its total witness.[65] Some may criticize much of the social and relief work done around them as undertaken for the wrong motives. Money may be given to assuage a sense of guilt. Service may be undertaken with an idea that this will earn merit in God's sight. Even the most saintly Christian may at times 'do his alms' in order to be seen of men,[66] even if those men are fellow-Christians who are expected to approve their brother's pattern of behaviour. But, as is pointed out in the section on the motivation for evangelism, none has completely pure motives, and the value of service undertaken from a wrong motive is not entirely lost. God who controls all things *can* work through a mixed-up servant, much as He desires clean vessels.

(f) Service 'until He comes'

Living as we do today in an age of violence and revolution, when even in relatively stable societies human culture is undergoing rapid and dramatic change, men are specially susceptible to depression and anxiety. Those engaged in serving their fellow men from motives of mere philanthropy or as part of a gospel of good works or utopian idealism may be led to despair as they see social structures overwhelmed or crumbling. It could be said that the Christian who has set his social service in the context of a Biblical view of God's world and of the whole Christian mission has the rare gift of being able to keep calm in the midst of the storm. Though called to serve society, he recognizes that his own contribution may be marginal and do little more than 'stop the rot' here and there and provide temporary alleviation of the ills of society. But the Christian's real trust, and real hope, is in God, who will in the end bring in His Kingdom by His sovereign power and not as the end-product of a long period of human effort and reform.[67]

So the Christian, because his hope is in a kingdom that cannot be shaken,[68] can be of real service both in the routine tasks[69] and in the crises[70] of this present life. He serves his fellows in a spirit of practical realism, impelled by devotion to the God Who is working out His purposes in the world.[71] The Christian will work for peace and for reformation. He will also work for the proclamation of the gospel and the salvation of men and women. He is called to lead a balanced life of witness and service, developing his special gifts and looking forward to the better hope ahead, when the Kingdom is brought in fully. He is to be occupied until the Lord comes.[72]

35

1. Gen. 1.31; Col. 1.16,17; Heb. 1.3.
2. Gen. 1.28; 2.15.
3. Gen. 1.21,25,30.
4. Gen. 4.10; 6.20.
5. Gen. 1.29; 2.16; 1 Tim. 4.3.
6. Gen. 1.28; 2.18.
7. Gen. 2.24.
8. Gen. 2.15.
9. 1 Tim. 6.17.
10. Gen. 3.16-19,21-24; 4.12; Rom. 1.24-32.
11. Ex. 20.12-17; 1 Cor. 6.18; Eph. 4.25; Mk. 2.27.
12. Gen. 4.14,15; Num. 35.11,12.
13. See especially Ex. 20.12; Deut. 27 and 28; Matt. 5.3-10. If warnings and promises are needed for the people of God, how much more for mankind at large.
14. Rom. 3.10-12; 5.12,13.
15. Ex. 5.6-8, for instance.
16. Ex. 23.9; Lev. 19.33,34; Deut. 27.19.
17. Isa. 5.8,20,23; 10.1,2; 42.1,4; 51.4; 58.6-14; Amos 2.6-8; 5.12,15, 24; 8.4-6; Mic. 2.1,2,8; 3.1-3,9-11; etc.
18. E.g. in Rom. 13.1-10.
19. Jas. 1.27; 2.8-12,14-17; 5.1-6.
20. Mt. 13.55; Lk. 2.24 (the offering for those of lesser means).
21. Lk. 2.1; Mt. 22.17.
22. Phil. 2.7; John 13.12-14.
23. John 13.15.
24. Mt. 22.21; 17.24-27. Cf. Acts 4.19,20; 5.29.
25. John 2.13-16.
26. E.g. Mt. 5 to 7.
27. Mt. 3.2.
28. John 18.36.
29. E.g. Mk. 1.29-34; 23-26; 2.23-26; 3.1-5; 6.34-44; John 2.1-11; Mk. 5.22-43.
30. Mk. 3.15; 6.7,13; Lk. 10.9.
31. Mt. 5.44-48.
32. Lk. 10.30-37; Cf. also Isa. 1.11-17; Jer. 7.1-15; Mic. 6.6-8.
33. Phil. 2.4-8.
34. Acts 1.8; Lk. 24.47,48; Mt. 28.19,20.
35. Acts 2.43-46; 3.1-16; 8.4-8; etc.
36. Gal. 5.22; Acts 3.16; 4.20,29,30.

37. Acts 9.36-41.

38. Mt. 5.16.

39. 1 Cor. 12.4-11,27-30; Rom. 12.4-8.

40. Acts 6.1-5,8ff.

41. Rom. 12.6.

42. 1 Cor. 12.11.

43. E.g. Rom. 12.9-21; 13.7-14; etc.

44. Rom. 6.12ff.

45. For a fuller discussion, see *Christian Motivation in the Practice and Progress of Medicine* by Arnold S. Aldis, being the Lister Centenary Address of the Christian Medical Fellowship, March 1967.

46. Phil. 4.8.

47. Acts 2. 45,46; 4.32-37; 6.1-6.

48. 1 Cor. 16.1-3.

49. Gal. 6.10.

50. Cf. 1 Pet. 2.13,14,17.

51. See especially Jud. 17.6; 21.25, commenting on some particularly unpleasant incidents in a loosely structured society.

52. Gen. 18.16-33.

53. Gen. 41.38-57.

54. Gal. 4.9,10; Col. 2.16.

55. Acts 10; Gal. 2.11-14.

56. Cf. Paul's distinction between his opinion and the Lord's command in his discussion of whether it is right to marry in various circumstances (1 Cor. 7). For a fuller discussion see H. F. R. Catherwood: *The Christian Citizen*, (Hodder and Stoughton, 1969), and chapter 3 of *Whose World?* by A. N. Triton, (IVP, 1969).

57. John 17.9-18; and the whole context of Revelation.

58. Mt. 5.13.

59. Lk. 12.32.

60. Mt. 12.28.

61. Rev. 11.15.

62. John 17.11,14.

63. Mk. 9.38-41.

64. Acts 3.6.

65. See page 31.

66. Mt. 6.1,2.

67. Mt. 24 *passim;* Rom. 8.21-25; 1 Cor. 15.24; 1 Thess. 5.2-8; 2 Thess. 2.1-12; Rev. 1.7; 6.15-17; etc.

68. Heb. 12.26-28.

69. Mt. 24.45.

70. Acts 27.22-25,31-36; 28.3-5.

71. Eph. 1.11.

72. See further *The Christian Citizen* by H. F. R. Catherwood (Hodder and Stoughton, 1969); *Into the World* by J. N. D. Anderson (C.P.A.S., 1968); and *Violence* by Jacques Ellul (S.C.M. Press, 1969).

4 The Motivation of Evangelism

As human beings, Christians do not act without some form of motivation. And the way they act is often influenced by the nature of that motivation. J. van den Berg has pointed out that 'the negative sides of more than one missionary method can be reduced to a defect in the missionary motive'.[1] For example, if the dominant motive in evangelism is a desire to 'see souls saved', then it will not be surprising if inadequate attention is paid to the development of on-going church life.

It would be foolish to search for a single motive as the key to an upsurge of evangelism. Though there may be a dominant urge, motivation is usually many-sided. The conclusion to which van den Berg came, after a thorough study of the history of missionary motivation, was that 'no one isolated motive or single factor can explain the growth of the missionary ideal: it is through a fulness of motives that the Church was thrown back upon its primary task: to proclaim the Gospel of Christ over all the earth'.[2]

One other preliminary comment that needs to be made is that the best of us acts from mixed and even tarnished motives. But the fact that a particular motive can become distorted and even blunt the edge of evangelism need not require that it be repudiated. In its place and measure it may be of real importance.

(a) The Great Commission

The obvious starting point is 'The Great Commission'.[3] The fact that it is paralleled in all four Gospels[4] underlines its importance. Those critical scholars who reject the authenticity of the Commission do so without valid textual reason. In any case, the whole thrust of the Gospels is in the same direction. As R. E. Speer put it, 'If you cut off the last commands of Christ from the Gospels that recorded them, Christ's missionary purpose would not be less clear than it is, and Christ's desire for His people would not be less distinct'.[5]

Obedience to this command was enforced by William Carey in the early days of the modern Protestant missionary movement, and it is widely used by missionary deputation speakers to stimulate concern for and involvement in worldwide evangelism. Indeed, it has been called 'the Church's marching orders', and it has probably been the primary motivation to missionary witness during the last century and three-quarters.

Yet the astonishing thing is that, as far as the evidence goes, the New Testament Church did not use the Great Commission in this way. In his valuable study of *Pentecost and Missions*, Harry Boer has shown that neither Peter nor Paul, nor the Church as a whole reveal any explicit consciousness of the commission as a motivating force. What we do find in the Acts of the Apostles is an emphasis on Pentecost 'as not only initiating but as wholly conditioning the missionary witness and expansion of the early Church'.[6] This is an emphasis that seems to be as absent from the modern missionary movement as the emphasis on the commission is present! Boer's conclusion is that 'at Pentecost the Church became a witnessing institution because the coming of the Spirit made Christ's mandate an organic part of her being, an essential expression of her life'.[7] Empowered by the Spirit, the early Church witnessed spontaneously; she could not help it![8]

(*b*) The Better Way comes from a Relationship

When it becomes necessary to stress the *obligation* to go into the world and preach the Gospel, then something is wrong with the relationship between the Church and her Lord. Boer draws a compelling parallel with the command of Genesis 1.28, and asserts, 'It is only when men try to evade or escape the law of their natural being that this law becomes a command for them. Then they must be confronted with the command in order that *via* obedience to the objective imperative they may be brought again to a normal observance of the law of their life'.[9]

Despite its hesitations about tactics, the early Church did not falter in its overall strategy—to preach Christ. Its relationship to the risen Christ, who, exalted to the Father's right hand, had poured forth the Spirit of witness (as well as of holiness) upon His Church,[10] made it a witnessing community. Instead of appealing to the command of her Lord (a procedure which can easily lead to purely formal obedience and even smug self-satisfaction) it was enough for her to act in character—to be what she was! The point was well expressed by William Temple to the Jerusalem Meeting of the International Missionary Council when he said, 'It is the very nature of Christianity that truly to possess it inevitably leads to passing it on . . . If we know what the word truly implies we must see that "Christian" and "missionary" are synonymous terms'.[11]

The resulting 'spontaneous expansion' was the order of the day in the earliest period of the Church's history, and it has been seen in evidence from time to time since. Whenever the Church lives in the power of the Spirit, steps will be taken to fulfil the terms of the commission given by her risen Lord. Spontaneously, she will rise to her responsibilities. Whether in her corporate capacity, or through individuals acting in her name, she will bear witness to her Lord in the energy of His Spirit.

(c) Love and Compassion

Another motive which can be distinguished from the foregoing, yet belongs to it, is that of love and compassion. This has its true source in the love of God for a sinful world,[12] a love which found unique expression in the atoning work of our Lord Jesus Christ and which Paul claimed as the motivating force of his life and activities.[13] A genuine desire for the welfare of others lies at the heart of any acceptable Christian activity.[14]

As well as being clearly visible in New Testament Christianity, there is abundant evidence for such love and compassion throughout the Christian centuries. Often this concern has been related to the *total* human plight of non-Christians, as in the early centuries. At other times it has been focused on their *spiritual* standing, with special reference to their eternal state, a marked feature of the pietist and evangelical elements in the modern missionary movement. Sometimes it has been little more than a *humanitarian* concern for those who are deprived of the benefits of a Christian civilization.

The motive of love, whenever it operates in human hearts, has an almost built-in tendency to degenerate into a manipulative kind of patronage. It therefore needs to be balanced by a strong sense of solidarity with those to whom love is being shown. For if we believe that 'all have sinned', then we as well as they (if such terms must be used) share a common alienation from God and involvement in human sin. We, too, are at the receiving end of God's love, and depend on His mercy and forgiveness.

Further to safeguard this motive, we must recognize the obligation which our own indebtedness to God places upon us.[15] This is far more than an obligation to make reparation for misuse of power and opportunity at the human level. (There is more than a grain of truth in the view that the modern missionary movement owes something of its impetus to a guilty desire to make reparation for the sins of westerners against their fellow-men in connection with the iniquitous slave-trade, not to speak of colonization.) Only as we realize that we owe a debt to God as well as to man[16] can love be preserved from becoming purely man-centred.

There are dangers lurking in exclusive preoccupation with the 'spiritual' element in the plight of man without God. It can lead to an unbiblical cleavage between the spiritual and the temporal. Neither our Lord nor His disciples drew distinctions of such sharpness, and the total Biblical picture is of God's concern with every aspect of life. The fact that first things must come first does not mean that secondary matters have no place at all.[17] The Gospel is for the whole man, and is relevant to the purely temporal concerns of life as well as the most 'spiritual'.

Another danger is that if we lay undue stress upon the eternal fate of the non-Christian, we may be led into unwise speculation on matters which Scripture has left imprecise. There can be no doubt from the Biblical evidence that salvation is to be found in Christ alone.[18] But the basis on which the eternal state of those who have never heard of Christ will be determined is not clearly revealed in Scripture. It is therefore a fruitless subject for speculation.

But if a narrowly soteriological motive needs to be watched carefully, so too does the purely humanitarian. Vague humanitarian ideals completely fail to do justice to the robust insistence of the New Testament that the gospel is a message of forgiveness, regeneration, and sanctification flowing from the saving work of Jesus Christ, the Son of God incarnate. The proclamation of the message—and the living Person to Whom it leads—was the passion of the Apostles. Neither active social service nor passive Christian presence, important though they may be in their place, can be a substitute for the setting forth of 'Jesus Christ and Him crucified'.[19] The solemnity of this task is well brought out in 2 Corinthians 2. 14-17.

(*d*) Self-denial

Sometimes the expression of love and compassion has been accompanied by an unusual degree of self-denial. It is surely significant that the celebrated passage in which Paul speaks of pommelling his body occurs in the context of evangelism.[20] Christian history contains numerous examples of self-denial as a potent factor in evangelism. Celtic missionaries during the early Middle Ages and men like David Brainerd and Henry Martyn are notable examples.

Such men call forth admiration and godly envy, but such motivation has its perils. Separated from love and obedience, self-denial can become an end in itself, and can even be regarded as meritorious. Since it tends towards world-renunciation, it can easily lead to a lack of concern with the Christian life in this world, and may develop into various forms of escapism. Sometimes those who appear to be denying themselves are in fact evading the humdrum responsibilities of normal life, or even escaping from or trying to atone for past failures. A refusal to accept oneself, in the proper sense of that term, is a certain cause of difficulty in establishing a healthy relationship with other people.

41

Though it may be evidence of real devotion to Christ and the work of the Gospel, the factor of self-denial is no more than an element in the full motivation of evangelism, needed to give it depth and seriousness of purpose.

(e) Extending the Rule of Christ

The Great Commission was given in the context of the universal authority bestowed upon the risen and exalted Lord. 'The missionary command', says Douglas Webster, 'originated in the exaltation of Jesus'.[21] The obvious parallel between Matthew 28. 18-20 and Daniel 7.13,14 gives further point to the observation. The conclusion is inescapable that it is by means of evangelism that the Lordship of Christ is to be recognized and enforced.

There is more in this than the idea of F. D. Maurice, widely held today, that all that is needed is for men to be told that they are 'in Christ' whether or not they believe it. The fact is that the authority of Christ, though bestowed upon Him by the Father and ultimately to be recognized by all, is sharply contested by forces human and satanic. Every inch of the ground has to be fought for.[22] What is more, the preaching of the gospel must be seen in relation to the Second Advent of Christ and the end of the age. Not till then will final victory be celebrated.[23]

All too often, preachers of the gospel have assumed that they also bring the definitive ecclesiastical, cultural, and even political embodiment of that gospel—in recent times, Western forms of church life, civilization, social structure and democratic procedure. The folly of such attitudes is increasingly recognized today. Since they have, to some extent, arisen from failure to appreciate the dangers inherent in the proper desire to extend Christ's kingdom and establish His Church on earth, some attention must be given to those dangers in what is, properly understood, an important motive for evangelism.

First, there is the risk of identifying the kingdom of God with some earthly embodiment of it, referred to in the preceding section. A related danger is that evangelism may become a means of aggrandising a 'denominational' church. The work of church planting and growth is vital. Some who have drawn attention to the danger of an excessively Church-centred conception of the missionary task have gone too far when they have asserted that the Church is a means to an end, and in no sense an end in itself. For, as Bishop Lesslie Newbigin has pointed out, 'an unchurchly mission is as much a monstrosity as an unmissionary Church'.[24] But this is not to say that the extension of a denominational church is a valid motive for evangelism. Denominationalism can be as great a snare as anti-institutionalism. For whenever sectional interests come to the fore, sectarianism is not far away.

Though the Church must never usurp the place that belongs to Christ Himself, it is dangerous to by-pass the Church. This has sometimes been the case with those who have engaged in post-haste evangelism aimed at winning individuals for Christ in every land, in an apparent attempt to push forward the date of the Second Advent. The note of urgency must never be lost, but in the past, as a result of this policy, the fruits of evangelism have sometimes not been conserved. We should presume upon neither the remoteness *nor the proximity* of our Lord's return. For all his preoccupation with the return of Christ, there was nothing frantic or slipshod about Paul's method of evangelism.

Granted provisos such as the foregoing, it remains true that the Church is under obligation to extend the rule of Christ by means of evangelism. To her has been entrusted the task of enforcing and exploiting the victory which her Lord has already won, the full fruits of which remain to be harvested. This is at once a precondition of His return and an explanation of its delay.[25]

(*f*) Conclusion

There can be no vital urge to evangelism apart from total commitment to the evangel as the divinely given message of reconciliation between God and man.[26] This involves more than mental assent to the message and the obligation. It means whole-hearted response to the love of God in Christ, and personal commitment to the Saviour Himself, carrying with it readiness to serve Him unreservedly.

Since God's love is directed to the whole world[27] and His redemptive purposes have relevance for the universe in its totality[28], there can be no question about our involvement in world mission. This mission is God's and He has entrusted it to His Church, which He has equipped for the purpose.

The Great Commission crystallizes our involvement. The Holy Spirit was given at Pentecost in the context of witness and proclamation to fulfil His promised role of bringing men into the Messianic kingdom of Christ.[29] It follows, therefore, as Harry Boer so rightly says, that 'witnessing is not one among many functions or activities of the Church; it is of her essence to witness, and it is out of this witness that all her other activities take their rise.'[30] It is not enough, as some have asserted, for the Church to witness silently by her presence in the world, or for mere dialogue to take the place of proclamation. The right to speak may have to be earned, and a sympathetic understanding of the non-Christian's point of view is essential, but if Paul's witness at Athens is anything to go by, Spirit-filled men must proclaim Christ as the unique Saviour-Lord. [31]

The very love of God which has been poured into our hearts [32] impels us to engage in sacrificial service directed to extending the rule of Christ in the hearts of men throughout the world. In this interim period, preparatory to the open and universal acknowledgement of her Master, the Church finds herself caught up in the global mission which has its origin in the heart of God.

Many forces combine to draw the Church from this. Ultimately, they stem from the enmity of Satan towards God. The reluctance of the 'natural man' to expose himself to hardship and danger deters many. The prevalent idea that all religions lead to God and that ultimately all men will be saved saps the urge to evangelize. The blurring of the distinction between Christianity and other religions combines with the growing influence of secularism and sacramentalism to blunt the cutting edge of the Gospel. All stand reproved by the New Testament insistence on the uniqueness of Christianity and the priority of the proclamation of the Good News. The Church's reason for existence in this world is her witness to Christ as the only Saviour of men and Lord of the Church. 'You shall be My witnesses' [33] is still the word of the Lord to His Church.

NOTES

1. *Constrained by Jesus' Love* (Kampen, 1956), p.212.

2. *Ibid.*, p.187

3. Matt. 28.18-20.

4. Mark 16.15-18; Luke 24.45-49; John 20.21-23; cf. Acts 1.8.

5. *Missionary Principles and Practice* (New York, 1902), p.433.

6. *Op.cit.*, p.15.

7. *Ibid.*, pp.119, 120.

8. Acts 4.20.

9. *Ibid.*, p.121.

10. Acts 2.33-36; cf. John 7.38,39.

11. Cited in *The Christian Message*, R. E. Speer (ed.), (Oxford, 1928 p.470).

12. John 3.16.

13. 2 Cor. 5.14; cf. 1 Thess. 2.7,8.

14. 1 Cor. 13.1.

15. Rom. 1.14; 1 Cor. 9.16.

16. 2 Cor. 5.11.

17. Cf. even Matt. 6.25-33: 'Your Heavenly Father knows that you need them all . . . and all these things shall be yours as well'.

18. Acts 4.12; Gal. 1.6-9; Rev. 21.27.

19. 1 Cor. 2.2.

20. 1 Cor. 9.24-27; cf. 2 Tim. 2.3.

21. *Local Church and World Mission* (Highway Press), p.66.

22. Eph. 6.10-20.

23. Matt. 24.14; 28.20b; cf. Rom. 9-11.

24. *The Household of God* (London, 1953), p.148.

25. Matt. 24.14.

26. 2 Cor. 5.18-21.

27. John 3.16; 1 John 2.2.

28. Rom. 8.19-23; Eph. 1.9,10; Rev. 11.15.

29. John 14,15,16.

30. *Pentecost and Missions*, p.100.

31. Acts 17.16-34.

32. Rom. 5.5.

33. Acts 1.8.

Chapter 2

The World As It Is

1. An Overflowing World

When William Carey and his Baptist ministers' fraternal set out at
the latter end of the eighteenth century to convert the world with
pledged gifts of £13. 2s. 6d, they tentatively estimated the population
of that world at 731 millions. Today, some 180 years later, the
world's population is thought to be in the region of 3,000 millions.
More important, it is increasing by at least 50 millions every year.

Part of the Creation mandate in Genesis—to 'be fruitful and
multiply'—has been abundantly fulfilled. But man has made a
sorry mess of the second half of that mandate—to 'subdue the
earth'[1]. In his misuse of his dominion he has added to the deserts, so
that he may soon not be able to support his swelling numbers,
even if, in defiance of all his past history, he were to share equitably
the resources of 'every plant yielding seed which is upon the face
of the earth'. He has destroyed the very trees he was given, and
tyrannized over the beasts and birds that God brought to be the
companions of Adam.

Only now, as human numbers reach unprecedented levels, does
the full horror of human folly and avarice stare us in the face. For,
while some of man's abuses of his mandate have sprung from
ignorance, more have come from greed. Immediate personal or
communal advantage have been more alluring than the well-being of
future generations: in the eloquent words of the Mid-West farmer
admonished for making his own contribution to the dust bowl,
'Posterity never did nothing for me'. Man has devastated, polluted,
and exhausted whole areas of the earth's surface in his search for
quick enrichment from minerals. Long ago, Milton bade us not to
be surprised at the presence of a gold mine in hell: it is, he says in
effect, quite the most appropriate place to find one[2]. Our world
overflowing with people now faces a prospect of attrition and
deprivation by reason of man's neglect of his responsibility to the
Creator who put him in a world of living things. It must pay the
price of his importunate sacrifices at the grisly altar of Mammon.

The pressures of population, of course, operate very unevenly,
especially in their effect on the food supply of different localities.

In India, at the end of the First World War, there were about 20 ounces of food grain per head of population. By the end of the Second World War, this had fallen to 16 ounces per head. Now it is even less—for the population has risen by more than 200 millions since 1918[3]. That is, the average Indian peasant has less to eat than his grandfather had. But even areas with a relatively low density of population may face difficulties from the swelling increase of recent decades. Sierra Leone has only two million people, most of whom are still engaged in agriculture, and an area of 28,000 square miles to support them; and yet for some years Sierra Leone has had to import quantities of rice, the staple food. The old pattern of shifting cultivation allowed the land to recruit its resources after planting until quite large trees could grow on it. The large trees do not grow now: there are more people, the same land is reworked constantly, the rest periods get shorter. And all the time, as the yield declines and the land 'burns out', there are more mouths to feed.

Along with the capitalist 'West' and the Marxist 'East' there is a third world where populations rise fastest of all; but it is not necessarily this third world's rise in population which puts the severest strain on the earth's resources. The affluent nations may make a more modest contribution to the world's overflowing, but they use an incomparably greater proportion of its resources and contribute incomparably more to its pollution. The exhausts of a million gleaming cars turn the Californian sunshine into a poisonous fog, and a myriad discarded polythene bags threaten to overwhelm the hygienic new Pompeiis of the Western world.

The human problems of an overflowing world are themselves diverse. The unevenness of population pressure means that some areas of the world could sustain a higher population than they do now, and may even seek an increase for the sake of economic development—and yet be terrified to open the door an inch to the peoples who are most in need of living space. For the latter, every improvement in public health or sanitation, every local triumph over ignorance, every breakthrough in technology makes more difficult the ultimate problem of the disposal of their population.

Another result of the dramatic increases in world population is that the proportion of young people to the total population has risen sharply in recent years—most sharply where it is most difficult to absorb. In many developing countries, well over half the people are under twenty years of age, putting the educational system and employment opportunities of these countries under colossal strain. The political implications of a large number of young people frustrated of their expectations are an added problem for hard-pressed governments.

47

We have, then, an overflowing world, overflowing to an extent never known before in human history. Some have concluded that within the lifetime of our children it will either become plain that the world's resources will not support its population, or that population will be reduced by endemic violence. Others put their hope in a greater 'green revolution,' or in the exploitation by technology of hitherto untapped resources.

But this growth is itself due in large measure to advances in science and medicine, fuller knowledge and better practice in public health, hygiene and nutrition. And the situation is complicated by the effects—perhaps irreversible—of man's abuse of his divine mandate to subdue the earth, his tyranny where God gave him dominion. And those who take seriously the command to proclaim the Gospel to every creature have also to take seriously the vast increase in the total number of those creatures; the fact that the greatest rates of increases are, and are likely to be, in Asia, Latin America, and Africa; and the fact that everywhere, and there especially, young people are, through sheer weight of numbers, counting for more than they have ever done before.

2. An Inequitable World

Whether or not it is true that in the foreseeable future the world's resources simply will not go round, it is reasonably clear that, as a present fact, they *do* not go round. The distribution of the world's wealth is far more uneven than the pressure of the world's population. And in terms of nations the dividing line in wealth (it is not a dividing line; it is a yawning chasm) is roughly that of the highly industrialized and the less industrialized countries.

One has only to compare what the *average* person can take for granted in terms of diet, amenity, comfort, education, health, leisure, and length of life in Britain, or Germany, or Australia, on the one hand, and in India, or Tanzania, or Ecuador on the other, to see the effect of this. It is not simply that some parts of the world are more favoured than others. Quite obviously the areas of industrial development depend heavily on those areas, many of them in the third world, which produce the raw materials, and vice versa. But raw materials sell in a world market where the terms are in effect fixed by the industrial nations, and the pattern of world trade makes it very hard for a poor country to be anything other than poor. A country which depends heavily on a single crop (as Ghana does on cocoa or Brazil on coffee) may be completely defenceless in a period of low prices for that crop. It has not escaped the notice of Marxist commentators that the world price of cocoa

48

(effectively fixed in New York) was very low for several years before the fall of Nkrumah; and that, immediately after his fall, the price went up again. Such a commentator might thus well argue that the fall of Nkrumah was engineered by Western financial interests, another piece of 'imperialistic interference in African affairs'. Such an interpretation is not necessary, and almost certainly not true: there are perfectly good reasons unconnected with Ghana for the changes in cocoa prices at that time. Nevertheless, it may serve to remind us that many Third World countries are virtually helpless before market conditions they can do little to determine, and may be utterly unable to secure their political stability or avoid their economic ruin. There is no knowing the pressures on the government of a small country of which cane sugar is the only viable export, when the government of a western industrial community quietens its farmers with a subsidy for beet sugar[4]. Not even control of a large proportion of the world's supply of a particular raw material can give an unchallengeable bargaining position: if the price of Zambian or Chilean copper goes too high, the giant concerns which use it can find substitutes for copper which come from neither country. Sierra Leone's share of the world market in piassava matters little when the world's brushes can be cheaply made in the West from synthetic fibres.

When, however, a country which produces raw materials wishes to purchase the products manufactured from these materials, it becomes the victim of the rising standard of living and inflationary economies of the industrialized nations. The price of the manufactured goods is fixed by the expected wages bill, profit and investment margins and dividends in the manufacturing country; and the country supplying industry with the raw materials will buy back its own products in processed form at a price fixed by somebody else's standard of living. If that country tries to reduce its imports by itself industrializing, the very machinery to do so must be imported at those same prices. During a period in which Ghana greatly increased its cocoa production, the result of the rising standard of living in Europe was that its purchasing power for machinery and manufactured goods was halved.

Now the nations of the industrialized world all, or nearly all, pay lip-service to the idea of assistance to the less industrialized nations; most recognize that in the long run, as major trading nations they have everything to gain from an increase in the living standards (and thus the purchasing power) of the third world. When united in international congresses like those of the United Nations Conference on Trade and Development or the Food and Agriculture Organization, they can recognize that they are in real danger themselves unless

49

this happens. But the danger is always in the future, the sacrifice would have to be now, and so really significant help is always to be given later on. That Mid-West farmer in the dust bowl stands for us all.[5]

There is, of course, nothing new in inequities between nations. The new elements we face are, in the third world, what Adlai Stevenson called 'the revolution of rising expectations' and, in the West, the dawning consciousness that policies which were once thought benevolent and philanthropic have in fact become a means of cushioning the mighty on their seats and filling the rich with more and more good things—whereas the declared practice of our God is precisely the reverse.

Our overflowing world, then, is an inequitable world, and the inequities show every sign of increasing and hardening. It is, moreover, a world in which the consciousness of inequities, and the presence of continual tangible reminders of them, and the conviction that they *could* be remedied, have never been so widespread. For the Christian mission in such a world, obvious wealth (a relative term) may be a treacherous ally.

3. A World of Nation-States

We are so used to the nation-state that it is easy to forget that it is a fairly recent concept. A century ago Germany and Italy had hardly and with great difficulty achieved recognition as nations rather than as confederations of princely states and geographical expressions. The First World War completed the break-up of the continental empires, and new nation-states appeared over the redrawn map of Europe; but at the end of the Second World War, only 25 years ago, a great proportion of the world belonged to the colonial empires of Britain, France, Holland, Belgium, Italy, and the others. Within the space of 25 years most of these have gone; only the Portuguese, and perhaps we should add the Russian, empires remain. In 1945 the United Nations had 50 members; now it has 126, the majority of the newcomers being former colonial territories which have achieved independence.

Few of them—and hardly any of those in Africa—had ever been in any sense nation-states before independence. The lines which form the boundaries of African states were drawn in the chancelleries of Europe; rarely do they represent the natural divisions among African peoples who had and still have their own groupings. These peoples—what Europeans have since the nineteenth century[3] rather quaintly called 'tribes'—have many of the characteristics of nations, whether we think of nationhood in terms of self-consciousness, of being different from other people, or in terms of language, history and culture. We speak, after all, of the English, Scots, Americans, and Canadians as nations, though they have a common language and the history of each is at certain periods hard to disentangle from that of some of the others. Even the Germans have a related language and an interlocking history. Such near neighbours as the Yoruba and Ibo in Nigeria, however, have languages more different from each other than English is from German; the history and culture of the Hausa and the Efik in the same country are at least as different from each other as that of the English from the Russians. The effectual cause of their all becoming Nigerians was the declaration of British rule over a whole vast area. Throughout Africa and in many other parts, the shape of the new states has been dictated by the shape of the old colonies. These had a history and administrative structure of their own and it would have been nonsense to attempt to dismantle it as if it had never been. Thus new nation states were born, while the previous structure, the nation-people, remained.

Most Africans thus have a double loyalty—on the one hand to the nation-people (which we call tribe); on the other to the nation-state. The first gives cohesion and a sense of belonging—and who can say that it should be eradicated? It gives a sense of a past, and no people can afford not to have a past. Yet it is also important that the second, the national, identity be developed in the modern world. It is an exercise full of supreme difficulty, and the wonder surely is not that there are tragedies like the Nigerian War, but that such tragedies have hitherto been so few. To talk as though the new nations were at an early stage of a process of evolution from which we triumphantly emerged long ago is not only patronizing: it is the crudest political Darwinism. The new nations are not recapitulating our experience, and may not necessarily have anything to learn from it. It is *their* experience, conditioned by *their* history.

The double loyalty, to kin and to nation, goes right through society. Most African societies have a built-in social security system, based on the extended family. Kinship provides both obligations and facilities: a boy may get his way paid through primary school, secondary school, and university by the interposition of a host of relatives: not just parents, but uncles, cousins, or simply members of the village. But, once a graduate, he is expected to provide in his turn for his kin; the children of his former benefactors may arrive at his home for education; his less educated relatives may expect to be provided by his accession to relative wealth with humbler positions which may be (or be thought to be) in his gift or his influence. Here are again problems galore for the educated Christian. He has not only a temptation but also a duty to promote his relatives' welfare. He has an obligation to help those who helped him. And how can his illiterate uncle in the village be made to understand that a gift—such as one always makes with a request, or as a mark of respect—is a bribe, and reprehensible? How will he ever understand a system which entails his nephew's promoting someone to whom he has neither kinship nor obligation, to the detriment of his own folk? When does the gift become a bribe, and when does loyalty to family and obligation become surrender to corruption and nepotism? And how does a man face a vocation to the Christian ministry if it entails telling people to whom he is indebted that they cannot have what they believe they have a right to expect? Some of us may well feel thankful that we have not to face some problems which confront many of our brethren constantly.

Perhaps it should be remarked in passing that the preaching of the gospel has itself had a part in bringing about a world of nation-states. Christian faith had much to do in many areas with the growth of new, wider loyalties, transcending local or clan or tribal allegiance, and in this respect prepared the way for a national consciousness. Often, it did more. Traditional societies were what van Leeuwen has taught us to call 'ontocratic'[7]—that is, power lay with authorities in which sacred and political functions were identified. Widespread allegiance to Christianity meant, however, that while local rulers remained accepted and respected, their sacral functions were in effect 'secularized'. It has frequently been argued that the Reformation in Europe provided the canons of thought which opened the way for the scientific revolution of the seventeenth century. It is at least equally arguable that the Christian expansion which followed the missionary movement was a crucial factor in bringing about a world of nation-states in the twentieth century.

4. An Urban World

For good or ill, one result of much that has already been mentioned—the population explosion, the diminishing living for the peasant farmer, the exploitation of minerals, the attempts to industrialize, the rise of nation-states—is that man is now living in more and bigger cities than ever before. A century ago, two-thirds of the earth's inhabitants were peasant farmers. A century hence, if present trends continue, hardly a third will live on the land. All over the world the countryman is giving up his long battle with the land and going to live in the town. The largest city in the world is in Asia. India, despite her huge surplus agricultural population, is in the throes of her industrial revolution. Nigeria has a city as large as Glasgow and half a dozen larger than Southampton or Dundee.

All this has a human cost. It is not only that cities all over the world can produce the most hideous living conditions, and the fastest-growing the worst. After all, people endure over-crowded, insanitary houses and indignity and violence because, generally speaking, they are better off than they were in the village: they earn money, or they hope they will earn money; their children can go to school. It is rather that city life strains to the uttermost man's faculty for social relationship, for finding a satisfying place within a community. Contemporary Western literature has much to say about the loneliness of the city, even in the vast chromium-plated, walnut-lined concrete jungles we have constructed for ourselves in revulsion against the smoke-grimed slums whose remnants stand like so many desolations in their midst. And there are worse dangers still. The presence in many modern cities of different, self-contained communities, some with access to amenities and privileges denied to the others; the development of reservoirs of immigrant labour, living in industrial encampments far from their families; the aggregation of huge unemployed proletariats, for whom there is no longer a living on the land and no permanent subsistence in the city—these all create a situation in which violence is endemic. These conditions can occur almost anywhere in the modern world, as locations as different as Calcutta, Johannesburg and Los Angeles are beginning to show us.

The new townsman is a countryman transplanted, often a countryman disorientated. His world of thought and life, his family patterns and kinship groups, his rituals and his religion were designed for country life, for the agricultural community, the struggle with the land. When he comes to town, they are irrelevant to most of the things he does and the things that happen to him. From henceforth he belongs to two worlds, and the forces which guided his life, his moral standards, his choices in the old one, no longer have the same effect in the new one.

The place which the city had in Paul's missionary strategy has often been remarked. In many parts of the modern world, for all sorts of good historical reasons, the church and its evangelistic outreach are essentially village-based. In the world as it is, it is perilous for Christian evangelism to neglect the cities, or to be insensitive to the conditions and needs of city life. Among past failures in this regard Britain might be cited as an example. It is a myth that the Church 'lost' the workers of the big cities: it never had them. It never had them because by and large it was not there. The agglomerations of ex-countrymen which became the large towns of the nineteenth century grew up while untold evangelistic and pastoral zeal was locked away in the rural parishes that were thought to be the heart of the nation.

But if an urban world presents Christians with a challenge, it presents also an opportunity. In the disintegration of his old world, the new townsman is often open to a new world of thought which would never have attracted him in the self-sufficiency of his old environment, where custom had an answer for every conceivable situation. Options are open, a freedom of choice is open, where individual action would previously have been unthinkable. In many parts of the world peoples who have long been impervious to Christianity in their traditional homelands are moving to the city, and there becoming Christian—or Muslim.

5. A Revolutionary World

The combination of some of the factors we have mentioned with some we have not makes—potentially at least—for widespread instability. The sources of this appear most clearly in some of the new nation-states. Not only is there the tension between the two loyalties, to kinship-nation and nation-state; there are also social tensions arising immediately out of the post-independence era. Generally speaking, in Africa, independence was won under the leadership of a Western educated élite (the product, by and large, of the grammar school, itself originally a missionary importation). In the pre-independence era this élite successfully challenged the European leadership in administration, education, and other spheres. If an African could do the job of civil servant, university lecturer, or headmaster as well as a European, why should he not get the same salary as his European colleague? And so European salaries and conditions became institutionalized for certain posts open to educated men only. In time it became increasingly the rule, not the exception, for Africans to hold such posts: and thus the educated élite emerge with salaries quite unrelated to the general income of the people. An income of £1,500—£2,000 a year seems astronomical where a labourer earns six shillings a day or a peasant farmer very much less averaged over a year's gruelling toil.[8] This might matter less were it not that so many other hopes of betterment by independence have been frustrated: increasing population and the continuance of the existing world trade structure inhibit any dramatic general improvement in the conditions of most people. Worse still, the swollen numbers of the new young generation have been brought up to better expectations; and bad times bring unemployment for school leavers, and all the ingredients of a revolutionary situation. Some leaders, notably President Nyerere of Tanzania, have striven to reduce the gap between student and peasant, between

54

town and country. Not surprisingly, this has met with stiff resistance from those who want to keep their differential.

Naturally, where economic and social dominance is associated with another racial group the incentive to revolutionary action is the stronger. But revolution is not the monopoly of one continent: a host of factors may produce revolutionary ferment, or eruptions of violence, in the oldest as in the newest states. There is the thrill of hope which change brings after static generations have brought nothing but acquiescence in misery, when, as in parts of Latin America, vested interests which once seemed eternal and omnipotent begin to crumble. Or there is sheer frustration—the frustration of minorities and their impatience with liberal assurances and promises that bring little tangible result. Who shall yet decide whether Martin Luther King's non-violence or Malcolm X's militancy has had more effect in bringing action about civil rights and poverty in the cities? Did not even little Anguilla get its roads and harbour in a few months of comic opera militancy—and would it have got them any other way? There is at least enough evidence that militancy works— at least in the short run, and whether or not it is worth the cost— to make it likely that we are entering on an era of revolutionary action all over the world.

This has little to do with any theory of an international communist conspiracy. There is plenty of evidence that communist countries are suffering similar tensions (though they may repress them more successfully), that communist countries serve national and communal interests quite as much as non-communist ones, and that communist countries have unpopular élites and frustrated minorities. There is also a recognition in the Third World that the gap between the professions of the communist countries and their generosity in practice is at least as great as that of the West. In a revolutionary world, the consciences of Christians, committed both to justice and to live peaceably with all men, will often be deeply exercised. In a world of revolutionary change, a world where change is the norm, Christians concerned for the preaching of the Gospel will not be able to take for granted particular forms of social or political institutions. They will need to be infinitely adaptable.

6. A Post-Colonial World

To speak of a post-colonial world is not the same as saying that it is a world without empires. The point is that everyone knows there *have been* colonial empires, and that they have gone. As a generation grows up which knows little at first hand of life under colonial rule, the consciousness that the new states are shaped by the colonial past does not diminish. It is of course possible to point to many items on the credit side of the colonial reckoning, but the new states will not forget that they were once colonies, and ugly relics will remind them. The sign now in a Chinese museum—'Dogs and Chinese Not Allowed Here'—will bear witness against Europe long after the acts of justice and kindness of individual Europeans have been forgotten.

When new states struggle to hold together their diverse peoples, they will recall that their boundaries were fixed by European powers. When their economies stagnate, or they increase their volume exports of primary products and get a smaller financial return, they will remember that their economies and their primary products were originally developed for the sake of Europe, that it suited the colonial powers to control both a source of supply for their own industries and a market for their products; and they will note that Japan, the only Asian or African country to play in the same industrial league as the Western powers (and indeed win there) is also one of the very few which does not have a colonial past. As they struggle to achieve a new cultural self-expression, they will be conscious of the more grotesque features of the Western cultural heritage superimposed on their own: botany text-books full of English wild flowers, poems about snowflakes where the temperature was never less than 80° in the shade, parades on Empire Day, will be recalled when the memory of the devotion of countless colonial servants, teachers and missionaries has faded. Indeed, a generation which never knew any personal affection for such people may well reject that devotion as yet another imperialist enterprise. The divisions of our world may be deepened by rival myths of the colonial past: the myth that a peaceful, orderly empire directed by just, benevolent, and infallibly wise Europeans passed into anarchy, violence, and corruption through greed and incompetence; and the myth of an evil conspiracy to exploit all non-Europeans, destroy their culture, and undermine their dignity.

But a post-colonial world does not necessarily mean a hostile environment for the gospel. Indeed, one of its most striking features is that rejection of the West and of its imperialism and its paternalism has not led (generally speaking) to the rejection of Christianity. The world's fastest growing churches are all in Africa, Asia, and Latin America, and in about every country in those continents there are more new Christians every year. But a post-colonial world has a clear message for Western Christians. In the first place, if they are to serve their self-emptying Master, they must eradicate every scrap of assumed superiority of race, culture, custom or society. In the second place, they must be prepared for the deep hurt of finding that people suspect such assumptions when they are no longer there.

7. Race—the 'Accidental' Factor

So far we have not directly mentioned something which has moved in and out of all the factors we have mentioned. It is potentially the most explosive factor of all—race. And perhaps its most disturbing feature is its 'accidental' character: there is no single reason for it, but many of the other divisions of the world as it is are accentuated by the fact that they are also divisions of race. The line between rich nations and poor nations is that of race; it is white nations, whether ostensibly 'capitalist' or ostensibly 'socialist', which have the wealthy industrialized societies; apart from Japan, it is the non-white nations which are left behind in the economic race. It is the non-white nations which feel most acutely the pressures of population, the worst effects of rapid urbanization, the severest strains on the nation-state, the most baffling sources of instability. The line between ex-colonial power and ex-colony is equally that of race. More tragic still, where white and non-white communities exist side by side in the same nation-state the same division of wealth and status seems to follow: whether the white community is a minority, as in Southern Africa, or a majority as in the United States, where immigrants from every white nation under heaven have made good, but not the Negro community which arrived before most. Of course, we can find a multitude of reasons for this: but, rationalize as we may, it is going to be increasingly difficult in a revolutionary world not to give the impression that there is not a sort of conspiracy of the — in the now almost hackneyed phrase — 'unyoung, the uncoloured and the unpoor', to maintain their present comfortable position against all comers.

Such, then, is our world; not as we would choose to have it, but as it is: an overflowing, inequitable world of nation-states, with vast and growing cities; a world of revolutionary hopes, deeply marked both by the long hegemony of Europe and by its passing; and with the interwoven complication that so many of its divisions are also, accidentally, divisions of race. It is in such a world that God continues to call His great multitude which no man can number from every nation, from all tribes and peoples and tongues. And, lest our hearts fail, it is worth remembering that there are now more Christians, in more places, than ever before in history; and that more primary evangelization is being undertaken than at any time since the modern missionary movement began; and that we in Europe live in one of the few areas of Christian decline. The majority of Christians are already Africans, Asians, or Americans.

NOTES

1. Gen. 1. 28.

2. *Paradise Lost* I, lines 688–692.

3. Cf. 3. M. Cipolla, *The Economic History of World Population.*

4. This is not, of course to deny the opposite effect of such arrangements as the Commonwealth Sugar Agreement.

5. Total British spending on overseas aid 1969: £211 million.
Total British spending on tobacco 1969: £1,695 million.

6. At an earlier date it was more usual to use the word "people"; perhaps it would help to return to the old use.

7. A. Th. van Leeuwen, *Christianity in World History* (Edinburgh House Press) 1964.

8. The examples chosen are from Africa, but analogous situations exist in many other places.

Chapter 3

The Church in the World Today

It will be understood by any knowledgeable reader that it is impossible to give, in so short a space, an adequate summary of what is going on in the Christian Church around the world. All that we can do is to highlight a few of the significant trends and developments of our time; and these predominantly related to missionary activities and the interests of evangelical British readers. Those readers with wider interests are asked to make due allowances for this.

1. The Setting of Today's Church

The Lord who brings us into fellowship and communion with His Church places her under an obligation to transmit the good news to all the world. The expanding, abounding witness of the first century Church enabled the Christian message to be heard throughout the known world, its first outstanding centres being Antioch, Rome and Alexandria. The scale of expansion through twenty centuries has fluctuated.[1] Stephen Neill reminds us that by the end of the third century there was no area in the Roman Empire which had not been penetrated by the Gospel. But distribution was uneven.

Constantine's imperial favour saw the Church emerge from the underground catacombs to official acceptance. Popularity bred superficiality, with a consequent lack of dynamic change in life and service. From 500—1500 A.D., a period entitled 'The Thousand Years of Uncertainty' by Prof. K. S. Latourette[2] saw great struggles outwardly with the barbarians and Islam. The collapse of the Roman Empire, the struggle for inner integrity, and the momentous advance of the fanatical Muslim faith during 500—1000 A.D. adversely affected the Christian Church.

Life began to generate again after the year 1000 A.D., and notable advances were made in Europe. By 1500 A.D. Columbus had crossed the Atlantic and discovered the West Indies. The Church began to move out with the explorers to new territories, and the West Indies and America received the message; but in the East, by the end of the 18th century, Christianity was far from acceptable and made few inroads in Islamic countries. The spirit of adventure led voyagers in search of new acquisitions. James Cook's fascinating adventures fired the young William Carey and others with ambitions to propagate the gospel in newly-discovered territories. By the end of the 19th century Africa had been crossed and recrossed, and the great exploitation by the white man had begun. Alongside the ruthless European land-rush the Christian Church moved in its forces to reclaim territory from Islam and to establish western patterns of Church government and denominationalism. (It is worth noting that in the mid-nineteenth century pre-imperial missions did have a halcyon period, one unmarked by some of the unfortunate features of the latter years of the century. For instance, there was considerable room for 'national' leadership: an African Anglican Bishop and two West African Methodist Superintendents directed affairs in West Africa in the 1860s.)

The second evangelical awakening, which had its origins in America, quickly spread to Great Britain. It produced an unprecedented dedication of youthful propagators supported by an equally new phenomenon of evangelical 'investors' who commenced the massive wave of international and supra-denominational societies. Churches with little missionary enterprise were left on the sidings as the 'express' of the new missions gathered momentum. This became the age of new societies. If the churches would not fulfil their obligation to the heathen, then awakened individuals, with little understanding of the theology of mission, but greatly burdened for the unreached millions, would go forward independently. By the end of the century the main-line Protestant denominations[3] began to take a belated interest in the thrilling enterprise.[4] Inevitably this movement was linked in the minds of many with colonization, and missionary personnel could not foresee the immense problems which would face their successors. Paternalism abounded, and patronizing attitudes were inevitably conveyed. Partnership and equality probably featured rarely in their dreams. They exhibited a dedication and sincerity which carried them through constant dangers and primitive conditions; it enabled the gospel to spread at an unprecedented speed.

The 20th century traumas of the Church in former European colonies must be set against this backcloth. That many of the churches are today self-governing, self-propagating, self-supporting and independent of Western influence and money, is one sign of the power of the Holy Spirit.

The contemporary Church is set in a radically changing international environment, far different from anything it has known in the past. Intelligent appreciation of these new factors is a most urgent need. Among the most significant outside of the Church, yet greatly influencing it, are those factors enumerated in the preceding chapter. In addition to these, we would draw attention to the following factors inside Christendom:

(a) Ecumenical Dialogue

This has developed steadily, particularly since the 1910 Edinburgh Conference, the stated concern of which was 'The Evangelization of the World in this Generation.' Discussion between churches and missions has continued with varying degrees of earnestness in the last sixty years. The great variety of traditions, institutions, and experience has slowed mergers and hardened opposition to organic unity. Theological factors and the absence of definitive statements have bred suspicion and mistrust. The emergence of indigenous churches in the East, unaffected by western structures, provides justification for hopes of a more simplified 'unity in diversity' which appears to preserve an authentic Biblical characteristic. Organized ecumenism is often seen as an imposition unrelated and irrelevant to the work of the Church at grass-roots level.

Inclusivism may lead to shallowness and ineffective Christian witness. The uniqueness of the gospel and its redemptive emphasis may be diluted in pursuit of numerical strength. If essential Biblical principles are compromised, this must inevitably lead to further division. Evangelical separatists, on the other hand, need to consider their position carefully. Pettiness and bigotry, caused often through disagreements on points of minor doctrinal importance, have made a strange caricature of the Body of Christ. Western churches must take much of the responsibility for exporting their own prejudices to younger churches. There is need for greater tolerance and Christian love towards those from whom we may differ.

Many younger churches in the third world have National Councils of Churches which are linked with the World Council of Churches, and some governments negotiate with and through such national bodies. Some countries will allow only such integrated national bodies to negotiate the entry of western church representatives or missionary personnel. Separatist evangelicals are therefore caught on the horns of a dilemma. Do they move in and work with the national body, or do they follow their own particular western church stand and refuse to co-operate with churches linked to the ecumenical movement? To refuse is to deny to many the opportunity of receiving Biblical truth.

Fortunately many evangelicals have worked happily and successfully, for example, in Indonesia, even though it is a **W.C.C.**-related 'closed shop'. There is a need to walk humbly along a difficult pathway, with a preparedness to acknowledge that our traditional positions may be vulnerable. Above all, we would call for a deeper consideration of Biblical truth and a detailed look at theological questions by the universal Church.

The *World Christian Handbook*, 1968, states that 'Since 1925 negotiations have brought 131 different churches together into 38 united churches through 44 acts of union. These unions took place in 21 countries on all six continents . . . of the 38 united churches 12 are at present engaged in further negotiations for organic union.' There is much to support the thesis that 'Union begets further union'. There is no reason to believe that this movement, with all its manifest difficulties, will not pursue its course, though its progress may well be erratic. Many schemes are under discussion at the present time. (See the *Ecumenical Review*.)

(b)   The Pentecostal Movement

This movement is affecting a growing number of Christians in regular orthodox churches throughout the world. Recapturing the spontaneity of the power and presence of the Holy Spirit in the Church, it is rapidly gaining notice, especially in churches where barren institutionalism has prevailed.

Nils Bloch Howell, in *The Pentecostal Movement*, writes:

'The Pentecostal movement is a biblistic-ecstatic movement which sprang into being . . . at the turn of the last century. The most outstanding characteristic of the movement is the doctrine of Spirit baptism as an experience different from conversion, manifested by speaking with tongues. The movement claims to represent a restoration to original Christianity, and has above all emphasized the charismatic gifts such as glossolalia and supernatural healing.'

There is a wide variety of opinion concerning the primary gift of tongues. Serious recognition of this movement is imperative in any responsible assessment of the contemporary church, especially in Latin America.

(c)   Break-up within the traditional, institutional Church

The growing unrest and unease of young people with establishment patterns is also raising fundamental questions concerning faith and order. This is far from being totally irresponsible. Our youthful world demands action; reasons, not rules; life, not death. In-experience often leads young people with incomplete understanding of issues to make naïve recommendations for quick solutions. They are impatient with the inordinate amount of time given to the running of the institutions, and agendas cluttered up with questions of buildings and plant. The radicals demand a revolutionary look at the real business of communicating a timeless message of hope in a world deeply influenced by despairing and often atheistic existentialism. A vigorous protest from young Christians will inevitably destroy unnecessary traditions and upset familiar, 'sacred', entrenched positions. Such a drastic process will demand grace and humility, but will surely yield abundant fruit for the Kingdom of God.

To analyse relative statistical gains and losses is beyond the scope of this chapter. The new *World Christian Handbook*, to be published in 1972, will give more accurate information than has previously been possible. We seek now to comment briefly on selected areas of the world.

2. Africa

In the second half of the twentieth century Africa has developed into a missionary situation of unparalleled opportunity. It has been calculated by David Barrett that by the year 2000 A.D., if present trends continue, Africa will be the most Christian continent in the world. The balance is shifting away from Europe and North America towards Africa and Asia.

Colonial Past

The contemporary situation in Africa has its roots in the colonial and missionary endeavours of the nineteenth century. To their credit, the colonial administrators brought more advanced technical knowledge in many fields such as medicine and engineering, and tried to establish a peaceful order. At the same time, they were seeking to exploit the economic riches of Africa, particularly in mining the land, where the white man's greed deprived many of their traditional land rights. The missionary too often appeared as the colonizer's colleague, linked with him in an attack on African rights and traditions and enjoying a higher standard of living than the local church.

Church and Community

It is always difficult when living in a particular situation to appreciate the total impact of one's attitude and actions, but with the gift of hindsight it seems clear that the devoted missionary effort of these years was nevertheless conducted on the premise that Africans were savages and all their customs barbaric. Thus Jomo Kenyatta: 'The Europeans based their assumption on the conviction that everything that the African did or thought was evil, a belief which is sadly not yet dead, if comments by white supremacists in our day are any guide.' The wholesale condemnation of custom, particularly in relation to the family and the tribe, created widespread resentment which still colours African attitudes to the work of the Church.

Canon Max Warren of the CMS once wrote: 'Every leader of the Church who has the task of sending men on mission must have adequate knowledge of the sociological facts lying under his jurisdiction.' There are areas where it is vital to understand African attitudes if the missionary task is not to be hampered. They include:

Race

The fact that Africans in Southern Africa are being oppressed by governments which would claim to be Christian and by Europeans who brought Christianity to Africa creates very real doubts about Christianity, not only in Southern Africa, but over the whole Continent and in the 'Third World' generally. Muslims easily prove the superiority of their faith by telling Christians to look at what Christians are doing to Africans in Southern Africa. The way in which missionaries and colonialists treated Africans as inferior while at the same time preaching Christianity, and the policies of white governments in Southern Africa today constitute one single stumbling block to the spread of Christianity in Africa. One member of the Commission found a large number of students at the University of Rhodesia refusing to accept Christianity because they believed it to be a white man's invention designed to make Africans passive so that they can be dominated perpetually.

Other Religions and None

One of the first objections raised against Christianity by more educated Africans (and these are the leadership groups now and in the future) is Christianity's claim to be the only true religion. In the face of Islam, Eastern religions, and African traditional religion, many in the 70s are finding it difficult to accept the claims of Christ. There is also a noticeable tendency towards apathy in all matters religious. As a result of popular education, materialism, and the introduction of civilization, Western-style, together with the widespread drift to the cities, there is a growing class of what are some-

64

times called 'evolués'—those who have passed from the traditional ways of life and thought of their ethnic group, and adopted Western attitudes.

Land

In West Africa the white man, because of the difficult climate, has not on the whole owned land or settled. He has done his tour of duty and returned home. In Kenya, Rhodesia, and South Africa the white man took possession of land by force or legal processes, not always wholly understood by the African parties involved, and began a settled life in which property passed from father to son. The alienation of land is not just theft of property in African eyes, but at a deeper level a sacrilegious act whereby part of the life of the tribes is attacked. For the African 'tribal land was ultimately under the control of the ancestors, and therefore inalienable. Its appropriation by foreigners was perceived as yet another aspect of the overall attack on the basic unit of African life, the family.'[5]

This communal and mystical aspect of land tenure is something that highly individualistic, materialist Western European man finds difficult to appreciate.

Marriage

One of the continuing problems which causes bitter resentment is the Church's intransigent attitude to polygamy. This is not to call in question the Christian doctrine of marriage, but to indicate that the presentation of the doctrine has caused and is still causing much resentment and grief. There are several criticisms of missionary handling of this problem: firstly, the speed and brutality with which the Christian doctrine was enforced, often with very little appreciation of how it struck at the roots of society; and also the lack of thought and action designed to solve the problems polygamy existed to deal with—problems of woman's position in society, tilling of crops, status, etc. Secondly, antagonism was aroused by the hypocrisy of many members of the mission churches, who were ostensibly monogamous but actually lived in concubinage. Mission attitudes encouraged hypocrisy, and some still do. Thirdly, the missions were led into error by their lack of faith in the Holy Spirit as the quickener of the African conscience. When one considers the centuries which elapsed before the Christian conscience in the west was awakened on the subject of slavery, which was as integral a part of society as polygamy is of African society, one can gain a little insight into the profound shock the sudden forcing of the issue was to African converts.

There would seem to be two fundamental principles involved here. The African convert receives the Holy Spirit exactly as does every other believer. The Spirit can guide and quicken the African conscience as He has our own, and must be trusted to do so. The missionary has the difficult task of standing back and allowing the convert to mature by a real exercise of freedom and responsibility, which involves the possibility of decisions quite different from the ones we are used to. The European church is not the sole possessor of final answers on all problems.

Scriptures

The formation of a mature African conscience depends to a very large extent on the availability of the Scriptures in the local languages. Some missionaries have an honourable record in this, and big efforts are being made at the present time. On the other hand, there are areas, such as Dahomey, where after a century of missionary work translations of parts of the Scriptures are only now beginning to be available in Fon, the language spoken by 50 per cent of the population. The importance of the vernacular Scriptures cannot be over-estimated. When one remembers the tremendous influence in Germany of Luther's translation of the Bible, and the equally dramatic effect of Tyndale's version in English, one can begin to see the vital rôle the vernacular Bible can play. Biblical portions are often the first printed literature available and many literacy campaigns are based on such. There is an incredible thirst for printed matter in Africa, but the churches are falling lamentably short in the production of attractive, cheap literature. The Communists are very active in this vital area.

There is a power of communication, an emotional reaction, and a spiritual dynamic in one's own language which is simply not there in a foreign tongue. The immediacy of impact cannot be equalled. The encouragement and financing of translation, printing, production and distribution of the Bible and of Christian literature in general is vital to the future of the local churches in Africa—and, indeed, in the whole world.

Independency

Any programme of Bible distribution may well have surprising and unexpected results. Letting loose the creative, active two-edged sword of the Spirit is likely to upset a few preconceived ideas. This has already happened on the African continent. There has been a fantastic growth of independent African churches in recent years. The upsurge has been greater in the last twenty years than in the previous hundred. There is an undoubted correlation between availability of Scriptures in the vernacular and independency. To put it bluntly, when the Scriptures are read by the Africans in their own language, they not only judge themselves but also the missionary by them. Ayandele, in his book *The Missionary Impact on Modern Nigeria*, says, 'Unrestricted access to the Bible, with its notions of equality, justice, and non-racialism, provided the early converts with a valid weapon which they were not reluctant to employ against the missionaries who brushed these ideals aside in church administration and in their relations with their converts.' This is frighteningly relevant to the contemporary situation in those African countries which make apartheid a deliberate policy. David Barrett estimates that in 1970 there must be some 9 million members of African independent churches.

The Zulu scholar Vilakazi, in an address to the Hartford Seminary Foundation, stated, 'The African is claiming for himself the right to interpret the Bible as he understands it.'

Finance, Missionary and Ministerial Training, Laity

This raises many crucial issues for missionary societies now at work. Some are moving much faster than others in transferring real power to the local church community. It is sometimes difficult, however, to assess how much hidden influence is exercised by missionary societies and boards in Europe or North America through grants, personnel, scholarships, etc. The question of finance is a particularly sensitive area, requiring great integrity on both sides. The giving churches obviously do not want to see money, equipment, or staff wasted; equally obviously the receiving church knows its own needs and opportunities best. Mutual trust in the years ahead is essential in this sphere.

There have been some experiments in recent years with scholarships for African pastors and students to theological colleges in this country. This raises the bigger issue of ministerial training in general. Is it better done in Europe or Africa? Is the curriculum too orientated to Western ways of thought and practice in theology and pastoral training? These questions could equally apply to training of missionary candidates. Half of a candidate's period of training might well be spent in the area to which he is to be appointed. This might eliminate wastage both for the candidate and for the indigenous church. How many African (overseas) churches are adequately represented on Candidates' Committees?

More and more within the African churches the women's movements, such as the Red Blouse Movement in Rhodesia (Manyano-
Ruwadzano), are developing and growing in importance and
influence. This undoubtedly reflects the growing emancipation of
women in Africa. It is particularly noticeable in the independent
churches, where many notable personalities have been women—
as in the Lumpa Church of Alice Lenshina in Zambia. African
Christian women are experiencing the same difficulties of recognition
as in Europe.

Politically the new Africa is either struggling with the problems
raised by its newly-acquired independence or else in Southern
Africa is still fighting to gain such independence. This is also true of
the churches who want to be masters in their own houses, however
appreciative they are of the work which has been and still is being
done by the missionary societies.

3. Asia

Great tracts of Asia have become independent nations since
World War II. British, Dutch, and French are no longer colonial
overlords. Anti-Western feeling is apparent in many areas and
is demonstrated internationally as they align themselves with the
Afro-Asian bloc rather than with the West. There is an insatiable
thirst for education and a renewed interest in ancient religions
which are adapted and harnessed to youthful nationalism.

With the colonizers came the Christian missionaries. Christianity
in India came as a challenge to Hinduism and Buddhism, to Islam
in Arabia, and to Taoism and Confucianism in China. For a century
the initial Christian thrust cut mildly into these systems. But all
too often the gospel was an appendix to the white man's political
ascendancy. Christianity in India has heightened the status of
women, given education to many, and concerned itself with the outcasts of society. But the Christian Church in India is a very small
minority; possibly $2\frac{1}{2}$ million out of a total population of 490
million. Anglicans parcelled out dioceses, appointed bishops, and
set up an organized church. On paper it looks impressive; in practice
it may have been 'premature or unsuitable and very expensive'[6]
according to Canon Douglas Webster. The contraction of missionary effect as the West retreats politically casts shadows on the
influence of much institutionalized Christianity in the East.[7]

In South and South-East Asia people in the mass dominate the
scene. The population explosion continues rapidly and the death

rate declines, due largely to modern scientific progress and education. Asia is young; in many countries half of the total population is under 21 years of age. Singapore now has 60 per cent of its population under 20 years of age.

By the year 2000 A.D. one person in every three throughout the world will be Chinese. They are already found in every continent and country of the world, dominating commerce and finance in every country of East Asia except Japan. China has produced people who are capable, industrious, intellectual, patient and resilient; for adaptability and shrewdness they are unsurpassed. Chinese Communism with its promises of racial equality and economic prosperity for all men is making a tremendous appeal to countries where appalling poverty and fabulous wealth exist side by side. Burma, Ceylon, Vietnam, India and Cambodia have experienced its onward march in a campaign to dominate every Asian country.

Resurgence of Eastern Religions

Burma is the centre for the new aggressive Buddhist 'missionary' movement. Missionaries in the training college in Rangoon undergo a thorough five-year course. Graduates find plenty of sympathy and support from Asian governments. It is estimated that one-third of the world's population adheres to the Buddhist faith. The emphasis of much of its militant teaching today is the failure of Christianity to achieve world peace. In presenting Buddhism as a force for world peace, Buddhists possess a most effective propaganda weapon. Burma has expelled Christian missionaries, and other Asian countries are not encouraging a Christian presence.

Resurgence of Eastern religion is often allied to a new spirit of nationalism, the test of loyalty generally being the strength of a man's adherence to his ancient religion. The Soka Gakkai movement in Japan, a fanatical sect with coercive religious conversion methods, is growing at a phenomenal rate. It is both sinister and challenging. The new face of Hinduism has lost its old passivity and is now militant, claiming one-fifth of the world's population. Ancestral religions are challenging the absolute truth of Christianity in open combat. Islam forbids Christian messengers to enter Afghanistan. To profess Christianity is punishable by death. In Pakistan toleration is granted, but it is exceedingly difficult to exercise Christian faith in a totally Islamic state.

Stretching like a beautiful necklace on turquoise velvet, Indonesia's 3,000 islands spread themselves across a territory 3,000 miles from East to West. Java is covered with mosques. The more adaptable strain of the Muslim faith in this densely populated island was probably brought by gentle Indian merchants rather than by the more militant exponents from Arabia. Considerable gains to Christianity have been realized in recent years, however.

Christian growth

The islands of Sumatra and Timor, together with churches in East Java, are showing the greatest Christian growth rate in Asia today. Since the abortive Communist coup in 1965, the Christian Church has seen prolific enlargement. God has been using vigorous lay leadership to further His purposes. Dedicated teams, trained and enthusiastic, scatter to the villages during the weekend periods. The Bible and Christian literature are in great demand but short supply. The pentecostal gifts of the Spirit are being used practically, and usually without divisive tendencies. Laymen also engage in teams with missionary personnel in tent campaigns and literature drives—as in Japan. Evangelism-in-Depth is operating in Vietnam. The Singapore Conference of 1969 gave new impetus to evangelism in Asia by Asians. Church growth in Taiwan has been significant since 1950. Much missionary manpower followed the fleeing government into this island. This concentrated effort has resulted in wider dissemination of the gospel with a resulting expansion and establishment of the Church; the proliferation of denominations and organizations is part of the price which is being paid for this.

Tribal work in Thailand, the Philippines, Taiwan and other areas still calls for missionary pioneers. Tribal people with their own clan culture have not always responded to an individualistic presentation of the faith, but there have been significant gains in the Burma Hills, among the Karen in India, and in New Guinea. Eighty per cent of the 200,000 Taiwan tribal peoples are now thought to be Christian. Disrupted by war, the eleven thousand tribal Christians of Laos have forcibly been dispersed to other areas; this tragedy has turned out for the furtherance of the Gospel.

Urbanization is a 20th century feature of Asian culture. Tokyo has eleven million people and is still rapidly expanding. The peoples of Asia are on the march to the cities, and literacy is increasing. The opportunities for Christian literature, and sympathetic intelligent radio programmes and other forms of mass communication are unparalleled.

In Japan alone it is estimated that over 52 million radios and 18 million television sets could be used as a unique channel of Christian communication. In the Philippines the Far Eastern Broadcasting Corporation beams out the Christian message to all parts of Asia in nearly 40 languages. Radio broadcasting in Korea continues to reach North and South, Siberia and Communist China. This land has experienced war with the Japanese and later with the Communists in the North, but this has not hindered the enduring progress of the spiritual awakening which took place in 1907. Greater gains have been documented in Korea than in any other Far Eastern territory.

Vietnam, much in the news as a result of the prolonged war, continues to experience Church growth as a deepening concern for others motivates the numerically small Christian community.

Export of Denominations

Roman Catholicism claims the allegiance of 84 per cent of the population of the Philippines. Protestant groupings are small and often schismatic, in many ways reflecting the independency of the more than 950 American missionaries from some 90 different denominations and societies (as in Japan and Taiwan)

Enlightened missionary associations accept both the principle and practice of oriental leadership. This latter course demands patience and humility, but it is imperative for Church growth, as demonstrated in Korea during World War II. The Church in the West must recognize the rapid changes in the East and pray to be delivered from the pride of any success of the past. The contrast between the affluence of the West and the poverty of much of the East adds to the problems of the oneness and wholeness of a truly international Church. Visitors from the third world no longer consider that the West has a moral superiority. The decadence and moral lostness of the imperial powers is often equated with an impotent Christian faith. Asia says in effect, 'If Christianity as demonstrated by the West is so lacking in moral virtue, it has precious little to offer us'. Moribund Christian religion has become a liability and an embarrassment.

4. Europe

For four-and-a-half centuries Western Europe progressively dominated the world. World wars, resurgence and independence of non-occidental peoples, and economic insecurity, have now largely wrested authoritarian power out of the hands of Europeans. Much intellectual and some spiritual power remains, but the age of

European dominance has passed.

Bishop Stephen Neill aptly summarizes the current trend of Europe when he says, 'Church attendance in Europe is everywhere declining; the lack of ordained ministers is grave in every country, whether Roman Catholic or Protestant. The secularization of life progresses apace. We seem to be watching a steady diminution of the spiritual capital of Europe, the disappearance of the old European synthesis of religion and culture, and a desiccation of the human spirit, as a result of which men not merely are not religious, but they can see no reason why they should concern themselves beyond the world of the senses.' (*A History of Christian Missions*, Pelican, p.565).

Christians in Communist States

Christian Churches in Eastern Europe have in the last forty years paid a considerable price for the growing tolerance granted to them today. The bitter persecution of Christians by the Bolshevik regime following the fall of the Tsarists has given way to qualified hostility. Evangelical groups, particularly Baptists, now share a limited freedom in a declared anti-Christian state. An irreconcilable hostility exists between Soviet Russia and the Roman Catholic Church which nevertheless commands an influential following in Poland and other Eastern European countries.

Although the Christian Churches in Marxist countries are living constantly with the threat of closure, their life continues and their strength increases. Herbert Mateer, recording impressions of an extensive visit to Eastern Europe in *The Life of Faith*, 1 August 1970, tells of the enthusiastic and virile life of many churches in Poland. Denominational barriers have been transcended as Pentecostals and Brethren have united in the United Evangelical Church of Poland. Persecution has become a tool of the Holy Spirit to unite believers. The idea of an underground church was hotly denied by the Polish brethren. Some churches in Russia are packed for worship services although other ancillary meetings such as Sunday Schools or youth fellowships are prohibited. Without personal witness, evangelism would be at a standstill in Russia.

Other countries in the Eastern European bloc have Christian Churches which are growing in numerical strength and spiritual stature. Training facilities for the ministry are however often restricted. One index of the situation is that from October 1969 to October 1970 nearly 750,000 Scriptures (mostly Bibles or New Testaments) were either imported into or produced within Eastern European countries with official approval.

In Western Europe, there is unrest in the Roman Catholic Church as the movement for reform gets under way. The great centre of Roman Church authority and government, where most monastic orders have been born and where theology has been developed, has been visibly shaken in the last ten years. The new interest in the Bible and the willingness to question old practices may bring a dynamic reformation in Europe never before envisaged or thought possible.

Protestantism is undergoing the painful process of violent enquiry. The anti-establishment mood is often a sign of unrest and dissatisfaction with barren orthodoxy. Within the confessing denominational churches, there are a growing number of cells, spiritual nuclei flourishing as they maintain a vital Christian witness.

Contemporary theology in Western Europe is groping in a maze of doubt, bewilderment and metaphysical speculation. Having denied a transcendent God, many are seeking doctrinal plurality without limits. Disillusionment is proving the theological student's downfall. As his faith is destroyed, he is reacting violently against traditional forms of ministry. The would-be pastor's assembly line has been broken, with an ensuing shortage of ministers. Against this should be set the development of confessional movements based on a definite basis of faith—'No Other Gospel', in Germany, for instance. See also Appendix II: The Frankfurt Declaration on the Crisis in Mission. Among evangelicals there is a serious attempt at new groupings and a developing unity—among the Brethren, Baptists, and Pentecostals in France, for example.

Babel of Missions

'Foreign missions' in Europe, mostly from North America, are diverse, often vague in their strategy, and suffer through lack of concerted effort. Missionary personnel hold varying views about European church life. Castigation of European denominations might be taken more seriously if foreign missionaries had some concerted practical doctrine of the Church to replace the old. Too often separatism, exported from Britain or America, has led to an inadequate concept of the Biblical doctrine of the Body of Christ on earth. For many years there has been a steady, faithful evangelical Protestant work maintained in countries where the Roman Church has been the dominant religious influence. Advances have been made.

Great Britain, traditionally Christian and largely Protestant, has suffered a decline of spiritual influence in the last 50 years. Denominational statistics record dwindling attendances at services and a steady decrease in active membership. Some seem to hope that current ecumenical developments will result in spiritual renewal and an upsurge of Christian witness. In the present climate, the institutional Church appears often to be wallowing in a sea of uncertainty. In many cities church buildings are gradually being closed and sold, rescued, in some cases, by immigrant groups with their lively charismatic ministry. The present denominational retrenchment will very likely continue, with more church buildings being vacated before the end of another decade.

The long-standing tradition of being a 'sending' nation with a mission to evangelize other lands will inevitably be eroded unless a new spiritual movement awakens Great Britain. The fundamental problem of missionary interest and financial support is gradually being exposed as societies seek support from a dwindling constituency. Too many societies are chasing too few 'customers'.

The crux of the problem is a hang-over from the Victorian era, in which societies took over from the churches the rôle of equipping, sending, and maintaining missionary personnel. The blame must be shared, with churches recognizing their lethargy in allowing this situation to have been created. On the credit side, British evangelical scholarship is now making an international contribution. Tyndale and Inter-Varsity Press are co-operating in making commentaries and theological books available in special bindings at low cost to developing countries. Scripture Union is helping its many-sided activities to strike roots and grow indigenously in many nations. The new FEBA missionary radio transmitter in the Seychelles is a British-sponsored and supported effort. Britain's contribution to the international Church in the future may well lie in a supporting role, giving specialist help to areas of particular need. Wide experience and Anglo-Saxon pragmatism, together with the dividend of a rich spiritual heritage, make this nation capable of a continuing world-wide influence for the gospel.

Although questioning of every institution is the pastime of youth, there is nevertheless a very significant response to the Gospel in the student world. Bible study house groups are mushrooming in many areas. There is zeal and enthusiasm on the part of numerous Christians. Church-centred evangelism is becoming a part of the scene. Church-going is no longer the accepted social pattern for Sunday, so a greater note of reality is heard in some of the congregations of Britain.

Many Evangelical theological and Bible colleges are full or nearly so, as young Christians prepare for leadership. Altogether refreshing, laymen's efforts are having an increasing influence in movements for evangelism and in the government and activity of the Church.

Worthwhile interest in the Church overseas is weak for a number of reasons, the two most pertinent being: (*a*) the failure of churches to proclaim the international nature and responsibility of the Church; (*b*) the inability of many missions to communicate with a youthful world. British societies generally have very few young men or women on their policy-making boards.

If evangelicals can resolve their present differences and petty sectarianism, the ground may well be ready for spiritual renewal. This could be helped through Christians from former 'missionary' areas preaching the Word of God with confidence and authority in post-Christian Britain.

5. North America

A report compiled under the direction of George H. Gallup Jr., President of the American Institute of Public Opinion, revealed that out of the twelve nations surveyed, the U.S.A. had the highest proportion of adults who attend a place of worship. It was, however, noted that the proportion (43 per cent of population) was smaller than it had been a few years previously. It is still falling.

America's largest denomination, the Southern Baptist Convention, continues to grow numerically, though most of its other ancillary organizations lost ground in 1969. Contributions to missions that year totalled £47 millions. Roman Catholicism has made spectacular gains since 1914. Protestants still dominate the American scene, but religion is losing influence in this massive country, with its intractable social problems. The effects of the contemporary environment are seen in the Christian Church. The materialist outlook breeds contempt, superficiality, and tragic separatism. New denominations or separatist churches spring up, the breach often being caused over some hair-splitting minor tenet of belief. The divisions are a blot on the history of a great people. At the same time, there is evidence of growing and organized evangelical witness inside the major denominations; this is happening in both Presbyterianism and Methodism.

Christianity in America is usually well organized and caters for the family, but growth figures may represent superficial increases and numerical gains are often at the expense of depth. One of Henry

P. Van Dusen's comments in *The World Christian Handbook*, 1962, p.52, is disturbing; he writes, 'The undisputed fact is that there has been no corresponding revitalization in morality. On the contrary, as the curve of religious interest has risen, the curve of personal morals has steadily declined'.

Statistically Baptists are the largest Protestant body, with Methodists in second place and Congregationalists third. Numerous other denominations and undenominational churches are found in every state. Co-operative programmes for world mission evangelism and stewardship are features of denominational life. Ministerial training varies in academic attainment and theological complexion. The Evangelical Foreign Missions Association (EFMA) and the Interdenominational Foreign Missions Association (IFMA), supported by smaller denominations and independent churches, operate a vigorous missionary outreach, with still increasing numbers of missionaries in service.

Impressive missionary enterprise continues to flow from the wealthiest nation in our world. How long this nation will continue to export the faith will depend very largely on the churches' growth in spiritual stature moving away from superficiality; and on the acceptance of Americans by foreign governments. At present, the dollar is often the key opening doors of great opportunity. This in itself may prove to be a hindrance if the spiritual roots are not grounded in eternal truth.

The United States as a world power will continue to be a major force in the foreseeable future, and her churches must inevitably assume an even greater responsibility for world mission Their rôle in the international Church has rapidly become that of senior partner. The success of this new position will in measure be controlled by the willingness to accept a less explicit leadership for a greater supporting partnership.

6. Latin America

Within the next 25 years the population of Latin America will have doubled, if present trends continue. As in many other areas of the world, the people are on the move to new and growing cities. For example, 50 per cent of Mexico's population lives in only 15 per cent of its land area.

It would be too ambitious to attempt an appraisal of the political situation, but two factors are prominent in many areas. Anti-American sentiment is strong, aggravated by left-wing infiltration. The second feature, which is recurring in so many parts of our world, is that of a vast gulf between rich and poor. In the last fifty years there has been an extraordinary growth of the evangelical church, particularly of independent, theologically conservative groups. In some countries the current evangelical growth-rate exceeds the population growth-rate. Such expansion is encouraging, but creates its own problems. The quality of church life in many areas is shallow, and the need for Biblical instruction is urgent. In a day of increasing opportunity, this calls for technically equipped men and women, including those who can exploit mass media for the cause of the Gospel.

The Religious Situation

For over 400 years Latin Americans, who are drawn from very varied ethnic groups—e.g., Spanish, Indian, and Negro etc.—have been dominated by Spanish Roman Catholicism. There has been widespread ignorance of the essentials of the Christian faith and domination by superstitious fear. Since the year 1900 this stronghold has gradually been weakened as Protestant missionaries with their Biblical Gospel, have penetrated this area, and particularly with the growth of the indigenous Pentecostal churches. 25 per cent of all Protestant missionary personnel are deployed in Latin America. From a strategic point of view it is a question whether they are deployed to the best effect. Romantic 'images' of tribal work are much more attractive to the ears of western supporters than the mundane story of witness in urban areas.

'In the whole Amazon Basin, for example, there are only 136,000 uncivilized tribespeople, most of whom live in small tribes and speak mutually unintelligible languages. Most assuredly, these tribes need to hear the Gospel but their evangelization must not be understood as the sum of mission. More than 250 missionaries work among these tribes, more than are working in the States of Santa Catarina and Rio Grande, which have a combined population of over nine million. A comparable investment in any of the large cities of Latin America, devoted to the effective communication of the Gospel, could produce more church growth in six months than would result from the evangelization of every member of dozens of jungle tribes.' (*Latin American Church Growth*, p.303).

The current atmosphere of revolution and violence has deeply affected South America. Missionaries have increasingly been working in an atmosphere of ferment. This has undoubtedly affected theological and philosophical thinking, especially for those concerned with student training. The effects of this movement are seen in a polarization; there is a desire for a politically orientated Gospel, or for a Gospel with no social cutting edge at all. The revolutionary atmosphere makes more urgent the need to replace Anglo-Saxon missionary personnel by a strong indigenous leadership.

Church Growth

Perhaps no area in any continent of the world has shown such phenomenal church growth rates. A significant feature of this expansion are the independent Pentecostal Church groups whose growth-rate far outstrips that of most of the other churches put together. 'This revival spread because of the active participation of large numbers of laymen and young people who established preaching points, house churches, and a large network of church schools. A Southern Baptist missionary executive, James D. Crane (1961), noted the following characteristics of the Assemblies' growth: (1) the leadership is Latin American; (2) the churches are self-supporting; (3) the structure includes a large community coming into the churches (whose average size is 48 members), and church principles such as simplicity of approach, immediate teaching of the converts, emphasis on the baptism of the Holy Spirit, and a commitment to indigenous church principles.' (*Latin American Church Growth*, p.151.) Among the more traditional denominations, such as Baptists and Methodists, which have tried to build on more western patterns, difficulties have been experienced, particularly when men in rural areas have been transferred into urban situations and consequently have experienced difficulties of re-adjustment to the more modern situation.

The indigenous Pentecostalists have developed their ministry from within their ranks through an apprenticeship system. The candidate receives his training in the local assembly, is tested there and has his call confirmed by the local church; he is then moved to a new situation, and thus the process of expansion has been speeded up. Pentecostalist enthusiasm and flexibility often meet the needs of the young people as more formal patterns fail to do. Pentecostals move naturally and easily in the streets and market places where people are, rather than expecting people to come into their shanty church buildings. The established churches have too often created a middle class and intellectualist image which has militated against church growth.

Factors Preventing Church Growth

There is an uneven distribution of missionary personnel in many countries in Latin America, but areas of growth are not necessarily related to the numerical presence of missionary personnel. For instance, in Ecuador there is a high concentration of missionaries and resources, but a low church membership and slow growth, churches having a ghetto mentality, both socially and religiously. The Spanish endeavoured to evangelize the Quechua Indians, often misunderstanding their culture and background, and consequently they found it impossible to communicate the eternal truths. There is a need for nationals to be given greater opportunity to convey the Gospel in the mother tongue of the people concerned.

It is a moot point whether the institutions created in Latin America by the Christian Church, such as hospitals, schools, and colleges, have furthered the spread of the Gospel or become a hindrance. In this flexible situation they too often drain resources of money and manpower which are urgently needed for church planting. A good illustration of this is found in *Latin American Church Growth:* 'Other factors may have contributed to the decline of the Alliance churches since 1945: (1) a rigid adherence to "indigenous" principles without the suitable adaption to changing circumstances (at the peak of the Violence, for example, the mission reallocated 25 per cent of the subsidy to a building programme, but then held the Church responsible for continuing all former programmes which had been financed by subsidy, a decision which the Church still does not understand); (2) maintenance of an inadequate ministerial training programme; (3) churches which lean on the mission, requesting missionaries to act as pastors; (4) insufficient sharing of authority with nationals. Consequently national leaders have charged that they are not permitted to solve their own problems or direct their work. Certainly much is to be said for the side of the mission, yet unless nationals have the opportunity of planning, solving problems, making mistakes, and administering, they have little interest in the enterprise. It is not surprising that, even after the Violence subsided, the Alliance has shown only moderate growth.'

It is obvious that the pace of church growth is affected adversely when the members of the local congregation do not feel involved and leave the work of evangelism to the so-called specialist.

The Rôle of the Scriptures

Bible translation has been one of the most important factors in the evangelism of Latin America, but we would again question whether this has been done on a strategically proportionate basis. Often much time has been given translating for small tribes in specialized linguistic groups, while much larger communities have been left untouched or with inadequate aids. The tragic lack of first-class Christian literature, attractively produced and readily available, has prevented the growth of strong and well-informed Christians, in sharp contrast to the many informed communist workers who are generously armed with their telling literature.

There is obviously a need to exploit the mass media of communication such as radio, television, correspondence courses, etc. much more than in the past in order to bring Bible teaching to the great majority of members.

F. C. Glass has reported: 'In dozens of places where I sold the first copies of the Scriptures the people ever saw, there are strong evangelical churches today. . . . It was almost invariably the case that the Bible was first in those cases where later came the preacher, except in those cases where, the colporteur being also an evangelist the Bible and the preacher came together. I cannot recall a single case when the Bible came second. Speaking from personal experience, I should therefore say that if you want to open up a new area, the first thing to do is to send in someone with a Bible.'

Latin America, from a Christian standpoint, is exhilarating, thought-provoking and abundantly challenging. Our reading of the situation suggest that more flexibility in administration and delegating of responsibility will be necessary in the coming decade if speed of adaption is to match the speed of changing events.

The opportunities for church growth will continue, but the speed will be regulated very considerably by the ability of missions to train and trust local personnel for the new situations.

The ongoing Christian movement empowered by the living Holy Spirit in Latin America must be deeply concerned with the social problems of the region so that the link between the life-changing Gospel and the social needs of humanity is made visible.

Chapter 4

Existing Kinds of Partnership

1. History of Present Partnership

(It should be noted that this chapter was necessarily prepared with the British situation in view; members of the Commission from overseas rightly point out that the use of expressions like 'our country' do not in fact apply to their home situations.)

It was not until 1700 that the first foreign mission as a direct product of Reformed Christianity was formed. This was the Danish-Halle Mission in India, fruit of the revival movement in Germany under the Pietists Spener and Francke and sponsored by King Frederick IV of Denmark. Up till that time foreign missionary work had been undertaken by individuals. Nearly another 100 years had to pass before the Baptist Missionary Society of England in 1792, the London Missionary Society in 1795, the Netherlands Missionary Society in 1797, the Church Missionary Society, the missionary arm of the Church of England, in 1799, the British and Foreign Bible Society in 1804, and the American Board of Commissioners for Foreign Missions in 1810 were formed. These were the expression of concern for 'the heathen' of the world, sometimes aided, sometimes resisted by the colonial exploitation of the various European countries.

Canon Max Warren, formerly Secretary of the Church Missionary Society, has said, 'The essential significance of the religious "societies" of the eighteenth century, and more particularly of the missionary societies, was precisely this, that they were "points of concentration", finding as their special vocation the responsibility to press the Church out beyond its immediate horizon to pursue its unfinished task.'

Most of the interdenominational societies, beginning over half a century later with the founding of the China Inland Mission in 1865, played a significant part in what Latourette described as the 'Great Century of Missions, 1815-1914.' These were similarly 'points of concentration' for evangelical Christians all over the English-speaking world and the Continent of Europe, particularly from Scandinavia and Switzerland. Thus, whether denominational or interdenominational, the Societies were essentially partnerships of European Christians, banded confessionally or doctrinally to 'Evangelize the World in this Generation'—the slogan of the first World Mission Conference at Edinburgh in 1910. That Conference narrowly pre-dated the First World War which was to accelerate the decline of western supremacy and the break-up of colonialism. Deliberately ignoring Latin America, it reviewed the great achievements of missions on the continents of Asia and Africa.

These achievements, apart from those of the Bible Societies, which during the 19th century had increased the number of languages in which the Bible or parts of it were available from 70 to 600, were those of missionary societies working in clearly defined geographical areas. There was an understanding among societies (the so-called Comity of Missions) whereby certain areas of given countries were understood to be the responsibility of certain societies. It was a convenient pattern in many ways; and for this particular period of missionary work, when those engaged in it were characterized by a strong pioneering spirit, it is difficult to see what else could have been done. The territories were large, communications were poor, and often the boundaries represented clearly defined linguistic divisions. As a result of these strenuous efforts a great harvest was gathered. Each section went about its business without fear of interference, planting either a denominational reproduction of the church from which the missionaries came or a church with no denominational affinity. In many cases these latter types of churches, without denominational guidance, have been weak in matters of church government and leadership.

The 'accident' of denominational allegiance throughout Asia and Africa, and to a somewhat lesser extent in Latin America, has been more confusing than in Europe or in North America where the historical and doctrinal reasons for the denominations are at least partially understood. A church leader in Assam confessed with dismay, 'We are now more denominationally minded than our missionary fathers. Before they came, we were divided into our tribes; now we are divided into our denominations—Methodists, Presbyterians, Baptists, etc.' The pattern produced by the accepted Comity of Missions has in many cases made inter-church communion and fellowship very difficult. In a few places, years of patient negotiation have produced Church Unions, as in the Church of South India, but even these have not altogether succeeded in obliterating the divisions created by Western denominationalism.

The 1910 Conference, however, served to force upon the attention of missionary leaders the great potential of a new kind of partnership with the 'younger churches'. The International Missionary Council, product of the 1910 Conference, and the instrument of co-operation between societies and churches on a continental basis, suffered a set-back at its 1928 Jerusalem Conference when, to quote Bishop Stephen Neill, 'evangelism was no longer in the centre of the picture, and liberal theology exercised its most fatal influence on missionary thinking'. From then on the International Missionary Council was suspect in the minds of conservative evangelical missionary societies, and when the International Missionary Council was finally integrated into the World Council of Churches in 1961, it failed to carry the bulk of interdenominational societies with it. The partnerships which either exist or are planned in churches and societies throughout the world today are largely based upon acceptance or rejection of the ecumenical basis of the World Council of Churches. Partnership between evangelicals in Europe and North America is subject to the tensions this division reflects back to the 'sending' communities.

2. The New Terms of Partnership

The 1938 Tambaram Conference, at which, for the first time, representatives from the 'younger churches' were equal in number to those from the 'older churches', focussed the attention of missionary strategy upon the fact that 'the Church itself is the great centre and the focal point of the whole missionary enterprise'. All future partnerships in the world mission of the Church, whether by denominational or interdenominational societies, were to be influenced by the findings of Tambaram. The Second World War, which finally exploded the myth of white supremacy and heralded the liquidation of colonialism, did much to force missions to end their paternalistic approach and enter into partnership with the churches they had created.

While, however, denominational societies have almost universally accepted the basis of complete integration with the churches they have founded overseas, the interdenominational and evangelical societies of North America (IFMA/EFMA) meeting at Wheaton, Illinois, in April, 1966, declared that 'the proper relationship between churches and missions can only be realized in a co-operative partnership in order to fulfil the mission of the Church to evangelize the world in this generation'. The basis of that partnership was then expounded in the further declaration that 'the missionary society exists to evangelize, to multiply churches, and to strengthen the existing churches. Therefore we recognize a continuing distinction between the church established on the field and the missionary agency.' In preparation for these declarations an Indian pastor was asked to speak on the need for this 'continuing distinction'.

It is clear, however, that the initiative for such structural decisions no longer lies with the Western missionary societies. Not only political factors, but also the will of the churches overseas is being exerted to make full integration inevitable.

By illustration, very recently (March 1970) the Congolese leaders of the Congo Protestant Council, formerly a council of missions, but latterly of churches, put through an amendment of the Constitution to transform this Council into the 'United Church of Congo (Protestant)'. This United Church body, while granting local autonomy to the various communities created by the societies, has made it quite clear that it will govern the priority policies and relationships of the total Protestant work in the Congo. It has called upon all missions to hand over complete control to the churches and to integrate into their structure and life. Plainly this has the support of the Congolese Government, and while there is no law yet forbidding the existence of missions apart from the churches, there is reason to believe that the Government will not look favourably upon such separate existence.

3. Integration

How far have societies accepted the new terms of partnership with their daughter churches?

As has been said already, the large denominational societies have for many years followed the policy of integration, so that the missionaries from other lands become part of the structure of the church organizations overseas, and it is true to say that now very few missionaries hold high office in those churches.

On the other hand, the interdenominational societies and some of the evangelical denominational bodies of the United States of America (e.g., the Christian and Missionary Alliance) stand firmly for the parallel existence of a mission organization alongside the church organization, a stand which was clearly enunciated at the Wheaton Congress by representatives of 222 evangelical mission organizations. The reason for this strong declaration to maintain the missionary agency is basically to prevent the missionary from becoming absorbed into church programmes which it is alleged could neglect the primary tasks of evangelism and church planting. Many societies either based in Britain or with branches in this land maintain this same position. An example of this which is often quoted is the Presbyterian Mission from U.S.A. working in Brazil. Having followed a policy of integration with the church, in 1917 it separated from the church under what is called the Brazil Plan, in order to evangelize and plant churches in the interior of Brazil. Once founded, the churches were handed over to the denominational organizations. William Read, in his book *New Patterns of Church Growth* (Eerdmans) says 'Partnership in obedience, as it worked out through the Brazil Plan, has been a sound principle', and proves it from growth statistics. The Brazil Plan was willingly accepted by the churches in 1917.

The question which affects us therefore as we look at the existing patterns is really 'Co-operation or Integration?', and co-operation can be seen from many angles: either the one extreme of complete separation, or a recognized parallel existence with the closest liaison and interchange of committees, etc.

It would be fair to say on looking at the activities of interdenominational societies that, while the majority of them maintain their own identity, they do require that their missionaries work either as members of the overseas churches or in the closest co-operaion with them. Increasingly therefore for those who maintain a separate identity, the societies are rapidly becoming service agencies to the churches.

The Overseas Missionary Fellowship, now an international missionary society with its headquarters in Asia (Singapore), receives missionaries from a number of councils in 'sending countries', both East and West. It is a fellowship of missionaries supported by churches and Christians in many lands. The missionaries in many cases, however, and almost without exception in Indonesia, where it is a Government regulation of entry, are invited by either local or denominational church bodies to work with them in a variety of capacities (e.g., assistant pastors, youth workers, literature workers, directors of lay evangelism courses). They are still OMF missionaries, members of a fellowship which has its distinctive character, headquarters, and regulations, but are closely associated with the churches. Some of their missionaries are still very actively engaged in pioneer church-planting activities, and the call is for more and more workers to be so engaged in situations where it is quite impracticable for the missionary to work under the direction of the church. The Bible and Medical Missionary Fellowship, which is not a church-planting society, but a service agency to churches and a number of co-operative Christian efforts, has a number of its missionaries working within the church structures of India and Pakistan. Discussions are going on with a view to closer co-operation between OMF and BMMF, and an understanding has been reached which may well point the way for similar moves elsewhere.

Reference has already been made to the situation in the Congo and we cannot but wonder how long it will be before such a situation is the norm of missionary operation. In 1966 the Regions Beyond Missionary Union had entered into a tentative agreement with the churches founded by it there since 1888. It was agreed that legal recognition should be accorded by Government to the church and not to the society, that all missionaries would work within the structures of the Church Association, that institutions would be governed by church committees and that all property would be transferred to the Church Association. A missionary committee, however, was to be maintained, first to attend to the domestic and welfare matters of the missionaries, and also to act as the liaison between the Church Association and the RBMU in its various 'sending countries'. The Church Association now maintains that the retention of the missionary committee is a hindrance to the government's granting the required legal recognition, and it must go, thus creating a complete fusion.

The patterns of co-operation are varied, but it is clear that anything that detracts from the centrality of the Church as God's instrument within any country stifles the sense of responsibility.

4. Partnership with the Churches at Home

Ever since the commencement of the era of modern missions, an era generally accepted as dating from William Carey's missionary journey to India in 1792, churches in Britain have played their part in the spread of the Gospel worldwide—first through the denominational societies, and then from the middle of the 19th century through the increasing number of interdenominational societies also. At the present time there are approximately 6,000 missionaries serving overseas from Protestant Churches in Britain in an almost direct ratio of two women to every man. Half of the missionaries are with the denominational societies, with the Methodist Missionary Society heading the list with 603; while those serving overseas from the various Brethren Assemblies number 586. The other half are with the interdenominational societies drawing their membership from the whole denominational spectrum. From a survey carried out by the Evangelical Missionary Alliance on a limited number of societies, the distribution of these missionaries reveals that the churches in Britain still regard Asia and Africa as the main areas of activity, these two continents accounting for an overall average of 65 per cent of the total missionary personnel.

The most recent statistics (1970) on missionary numbers have just been issued by the Missions Advanced Research and Communication Centre in the U.S.A. This puts the total missionary force throughout the world as between 45,000 and 50,000, of whom 33,290 (approximately 70 per cent) are from North America. Latin America has gradually been gaining priority over Asia and Africa as the chief area of missionary activity from North America, and the 1970 statistics confirm that 32 per cent of North American Protestant missionaries now serve in countries of Latin America, 29 per cent in Asia and about 25 per cent in Africa. If the total figure of between 45,000 and 50,000 is correct, then Britain's approximately 6,000 missionaries make up about 40 per cent of the missionary strength of the remainder of the world apart from North America, and about 13 per cent of the world total. The *World Christian Handbook* of 1968 puts the total Protestant communities of Asia, Africa, and South America as $18\frac{1}{2}$ million, $21\frac{1}{2}$ million and $10\frac{1}{2}$ million respectively amid populations which in 1967 were 1,830 million, 306 million, and 170 million respectively. It will be seen therefore that the missionary societies of Britain and of the West generally consider that their main force must still be expended upon those three great areas where the churches are the product of their 150 years of effort.

It is difficult to draw conclusions from these statistics, although we must be very grateful to those who have compiled them. So far it seems plain that the 'overseas missionary activities' of the churches in Asia, Africa, and Latin America are very small, but perhaps the new Handbook will begin to show that continents like Africa and Latin America, where in certain places the churches are growing faster than the population, are beginning to move with the world-wide missionary concern that has characterized the churches of Europe and North America for over a century and a half. *Asia Focus*, second quarter 1970, reports that 'there are probably about 150 Asian missionaries, including wives, at work in other countries of Asia. . . . Outside this listing there are at least as many again who have been sent by churches or Christian agencies outside the membership of the EACC'. The report goes on to comment on the trends indicated at present in this development, and is worth careful study.

But what is the measure of this partnership so far as churches in Britain are concerned?

How seriously is this partnership taken? As the Churches of the Evangelical Church of Westphalia in Germany were stimulated to fresh interest in overseas missionary work, their District Synod in 1957 included this within a number of resolutions—'We are willing to continue to channel our love and service for missions through the missionary societies, as long as they understand that they are the deputies and executives of the missionary activity of the church and her parishes.'

In its recent survey, the EMA has been attempting to discover the degree of realization of this partnership on the part of evangelical churches in Britain. From replies received from 610 church leaders out of a total of 4,000 from all over the country, it was discovered that there was an average of 1.2 missionaries overseas from every church, while 0.5 members from each church were overseas in a secular capacity, and a further 0.2 from each church were in training for missionary service. 72 per cent of the churches had no men members in missionary service, while 64 per cent had no women members in such service. 17 per cent had one man, and 20 per cent one women, while only 2 per cent had four or more men and 4 per cent had 4 or more women. From the angle of giving, 28 per cent of the churches gave about 15 per cent of their total income to missionary work, while at the extreme ends 18 per cent gave about 5 per cent and 6 per cent gave 40 per cent or more. In answer to an attempt to discover the degree of missionary interest, the following percentages were attached to the four suggested attitudes.

What is the common attitude towards missionary work in your Church?
1. An extension of their own witness here at home: 34 per cent
2. An optional extra for those with plenty of time: 23 per cent
3. A duty, but rather a nuisance: 21 per cent
4. No longer the concern of the Western Church: 16 per cent
   Unspecified: 6 per cent

The size of the first group may partly be accounted for in the fact that 59 per cent of the church leaders only occasionally introduced missionary topics into their regular services, where as 34 per cent introduced them weekly into their Bible study or prayer meetings.

The EMA survey has clearly revealed that missionary interest in churches is very closely linked with a personal knowledge of an individual missionary. 55 per cent of church attenders, for instance, put personal interest in a missionary as their reason for missionary interest, and this personal interest encouraged them to pray more and to give more. Anglicans would probably agree that their promotion of the 'link' missionary, whereby a church is linked with a specific missionary for interest, prayer, and gift, has been more successful than the promotion of 'mutual responsibility and interdependence' (MRI) whereby a diocese in this country became linked with and interested in a diocese overseas. This latter does not have the same personal element as the 'link missionary'. However, it does suggest that when the 'foreign missionary' is no longer on 'the field' it is going to be extremely difficult to maintain the interest of churches in Britain in the life of churches overseas.

It is true that for the greater part of the membership of British churches the life and work of churches overseas is not very important. There are many who feel that the task of evangelism in the British Isles demands all or the greater part of our energies. To them it seems more important to preach the Gospel effectively here than to export preachers to other lands. To such it must be said that, whereas we realize that opportunities and needs exist everywhere, it is for churches in this country to look out upon the world, and give fellowship and help in places where a pooling of our resources could make a big difference to a movement overseas which is plainly of the Holy Spirit.

If the churches in Britain are genuinely dissatisfied with the terms of partnership extended to them by the missionary societies, if they feel that these societies need restructuring for a more realistic tackling of the task overseas, then let them call upon the societies to meet them in a conference or series of conferences in which influential members of the churches can face the issues of world mission with the societies. Such conferences may well produce structures and plans which will be more representative of the churches' missionary incentives and efforts for this day of opportunity, and could be one beneficial outcome of this Report.

5. Partnership between Societies at Home

If we accept Max Warren's definition of the societies as 'points of concentration' for the churches, we must give some thought to the operation of those societies in this partnership. In the EMA survey a professor of electronics emphasized the place of the societies when answering a question 'Should society-based work be replaced by church-based work?'. He said 'At the present time the societies are centres of Christian life and activity'. This was really an exhortation to put all that we can into the initiatives of the societies; in other words, for Christians in all the churches to come to these 'points of concentration' for a particular work with which God has burdened us and pour all their resources and efforts into it.

In no instance is this so clearly seen as in the 'specialist societies' which serve churches, and in their worldwide endeavour in a particular medium. Their claim for partnership from the churches is almost unchallenged, and we have seen great achievements through them. The British and Foreign Bible Society, associated with other national bodies worldwide in the United Bible Societies, provides the Bible for Britain and virtually every other country of the world. The Scripture Gift Mission stands unique in Britain both by the extent of its outreach in Scripture portions, and by its generous grants to workers in all lands through the fellowship of those who give to it. Similarly the Scripture Union organization, with its concentration upon Bible study helps and young people's work, provides a growing platform for partnership from Christians of all Protestant churches in many lands today. In the field of literature the United Society for Christian Literature and the Christian Literature Crusade in their different spheres are showing what joint action can accomplish. In another sphere altogether the Leprosy Mission, which began with the concern of a Britisher in India, has grown into a worldwide partnership dedicated to the Christian care of the leprosy patient and the eradication of this dreaded disease. The Commission would commend a careful study of the reports and accounts of these bodies as demonstrating what concentrated partnership can achieve, and as evidence of what might be achieved if some of the many smaller efforts by a multitude of societies were brought together into a combined operation in the home countries. We are at the beginning of the first real partnership in radio work on the part of the Far East Broadcasting Associates in Britain. This is a concentrated effort, on the part of those for whom missionary radio is a priority, to influence for Christ the whole of the Indian sub-continent, the Middle East and Eastern and Southern Africa.

There are two bodies in Britain to whose existence a passing reference has been made in this chapter when talking of the integration of the International Missionary Council into the World Council of Churches.

The British branch of the IMC is the Conference of Missionary Societies of Great Britain, which is playing its full part in the WCC's Division of World Mission and Evangelism's policy of 'Joint Action for Mission'. Member societies of this Conference have achieved a real understanding of co-operative effort, both geographically and functionally in assisting the churches overseas which have been brought into being by their work. The main denominational societies plainly dominate this Conference by their united financial support and by their full commitment to the ecumenical objectives of the World Council of Churches. Some evangelical and inter-denominational societies retain membership in the Conference, although separating themselves from the operations and budget of the World Council. No account, however brief, of the activities of the World Council of Churches would be complete without reference to the achievements of the Theological Education Fund, from which many evangelical institutions have also benefitted: Christian Aid, responsible for the relief of people in need all over the world; and also its newly organized department of Christian Preparation for Work Abroad to which the Commission's section on the non-professional missionary refers. The Conference also works closely with the British Council of Churches, and they recently conducted a joint twelve-month effort to stimulate concern for mission at home and overseas in the churches of Britain.

The Evangelical Missionary Alliance, founded in 1957, brings together some 70 evangelical societies and Bible and Missionary Training Colleges. Its real usefulness has been in drawing the executives of the Societies and Colleges into frequent discussion and study, making them aware of each other and revealing the potential, at least, of close co-operation. For the first time, Societies in the EMA have been able to look together at the needs of a geographical or ethnic area and plan accordingly, and some of the walls of partition are beginning to crumble or at least to be seen as disposable. The time may not be far distant when, through the partnership in the EMA, the churches of this country will be presented with the needs and opportunities of a given continent by a united voice and in a united operation. The Evangelical Missionary Alliance was sponsored by the Evangelical Alliance, a body which has stood for united effort on strategic issues since 1846, and there are strengthening ties of active association between the EA and the EMA. This is not least through The Evangelical Alliance Relief (TEAR) Fund, which is a growing 'point of concentration' for the compassionate expression of evangelicals' concern for those in distress, particularly in areas where EMA Societies are at work.

6. Partnership in Training

The 'missionary', the one to be sent by one part of the Church to another part of the Church, from one country to another, is still a very important member of the existing partnership patterns. His very title 'missionary' is questioned; it is under suspicion because of its colonial associations in the minds of people in newly independent countries; it is questioned, too, because it seems to infer some kind of extra-ecclesiastical office which automatically holds greater honour and privilege than any local ecclesiastical office. The Commission recognizes this difficulty but does not feel able to find a more suitable name! (The General Director of the Overseas Missionary Fellowship suggests 'Internationals' as an alternative.) It prefers to concentrate on the thought that those who are going, who are being sent to or who are being received from other lands for training, need to be taught how best to exercise the gift received from the Spirit for ministry. Our existing partnerships between churches, societies and colleges recognize the need to adapt themselves and their relationship to accommodate new categories of missionaries. There are still the full-time evangelists, Bible teachers, the professional, medical, and educational workers, but today there are also the aeroplane pilots and mechanics, the journalists, the dramatists, the radio operators and engineers, the office workers, and the business and bookshop managers: there are those who go out with the missionary society; those who go directly into the service of churches overseas; those who go into secular or Government employ. Each has a different task, each has a different set of professional priorities, but all have a common aim, to fulfil a missionary vocation overseas. Primarily churches are the second member of the partnership, the place where the potential missionary first realizes that potential by local training, which includes fellowship, teaching, encouragement, service and commendation. Vital fellowship, we have seen, often breaks down because a trainee, a candidate, or a missionary has not the backing of a local church at home. The training college usually receives the trainee from the local church and prepares him for service with the fourth member of the partnership, the society. The Commission recognizes that there is need for much closer liaison between the society and the college, that both may know, and the trainee himself know, what he or she is being trained for.

Training Overseas Students in British Colleges

Increasingly, the Church in this country (and this applies to other countries, too) is being asked to show its relationship to and concern for the Church overseas by undertaking the theological or Bible training of some of its members. This is becoming an accepted pattern. The Commission asked one of its members to carry out a survey on a number of students from overseas churches in this country. Being such a student himself he was able to do this more effectively. We summarize here his findings.

He studied 170 students (140 men: 30 women); 110 from Africa and 54 from Asia, again reflecting that these two continents are dominant in British missionary effort. 60 per cent (93) of the students went to 13 Bible and Missionary Training Colleges: the other 40 per cent (77) went to seven Theological Colleges.

(a) Bible and Missionary Training Colleges

Of the 93 at these colleges 55 per cent had no academic qualification before entering, yet of these 55 per cent, college diplomas were gained by 80 per cent. 40 per cent had either graduate or teacher's qualifications or some professional qualification and 88 per cent of these gained the college diploma.

(b) Theological Colleges

Of the 77 students only 10 had no qualification and yet in the BD or Dip.Th. exams only 37.5 per cent were successful. The majority were described as unsuitable academically, but were, with few exceptions, of good character, with a genuine Christian faith and a great potential for Christian work.

Of the 170 students eight became missionaries to countries other than their own, including two, one from Ceylon and another from West Indies, who are missionaries to England.

The achievement of men at Bible and Missionary Colleges by far surpasses that at Theological Colleges: the reason seems to be the fact that the courses offered were suited to the needs and abilities of the students and were directly relevant to the situation in their own countries. Generally the Theological Colleges are not suited to training overseas students for the needs of their home churches. The fact that the students were, for the most part, separated from their families may have been another factor causing anxiety and stress.

The survey underlines the need for greater selectivity in order to ensure greater success for this very valuable aspect of partnership. Students should be discouraged from taking courses for which they are not qualified. There is no doubt, however, that the training of overseas students in evangelical colleges in this country has been a valuable partnership between churches here and overseas especially during the past six years. The partnership should be continued, provided the Colleges take students who are already well qualified, whether they are laymen or clergy: the idea that clergy are more suited to theological training does not seem to have statistical support!

The study then makes an important point which underlines some of the current experiments in theological education being carried out between 'missionaries' and 'nationals' overseas. It says, 'Though receiving students here from overseas is an advantage not only to the students, but also to the life of the colleges, it should be realized that many more problems would be overcome if there were suitable theological and missionary colleges in the developing countries. It is therefore important to encourage evangelical theologians from Britain and elsewhere to offer their services in existing theological colleges overseas as well as in the university faculties of religious studies. Where no suitable colleges exist, the churches here could establish and support such colleges'.

Recently the World Evangelical Fellowship has started its Theological Assistance Programme, and one of its chief concerns is to make available evangelical theologians from Britain and other countries both to give lectures in colleges overseas and to conduct theological conferences. Member Societies within the EMA have already discussed within their Continental groups the possibility of better staffing and upgrading of Bible Schools and theological colleges within the areas they serve.

But this is a good point to move from the situation at home in Britain to look at partnerships that exist overseas, for it is in the realm of theological education, among other things, that some progress has been made.

7. Partnership Overseas

Reference has already been made to the 'Comity of Missions' which, while it negatively kept missions apart, from a positive angle was also an agreement or understanding. Most partnerships depend upon understanding and agreement. In most countries, the national Christian Councils were the local branch of the International Missionary Council and tried to push along the idea of partnership that emanated from the 1910 Conference in Edinburgh. In the first place, these Councils were composed largely of missionary societies, but are now generally Councils of Churches. They were the sponsors and to some extent the protectors of the Comity arrangements. Following the IMC 1938 Tambaran Conference, some—the Christian Council of India was an example—did their best to justify the continuance or otherwise of the Comity plans by a survey of how each mission was really evangelizing its area. This led to consultations on evangelism and the production of common study material. The Councils by common consent assumed collective responsibility for such things as representation to government: medical associations were formed by the Council membership to promote common standards of work. Some Councils were used as distributors of Government subsidies for education. In spite therefore of Comity Christians became aware of each other across their denominational partitions. The church unity movement, however, which some of the Councils, even in their missionary-dominated phases, tried to promote, has met with limited success. The Church of South India was formed in 1947 after almost half a century of negotiation; as this Commission makes its Report, the United Church of North India, although achieving fulfilment, failed to meet the objections of the most influential negotiating church, and thus lost half its total potential membership.

The so-called 'horizontal' unity of an organic nature (that is, for instance, from a Baptist Union in one country to other Baptist Unions in the Baptist World Alliance) is easier to achieve than 'vertical' unity between one denomination and another in a given country. For instance, the Council of Churches in Indonesia has tried unsuccessfully for years to achieve Church unity there. Recent developments in Congo may point to a different way forward.

In the midst of great communities of non-Christians, the urge to partnership always seems stronger overseas and there has been a real degree of evangelical co-operation. The World Council of Churches at its New Delhi Assembly in 1961 absorbed the International Missionary Council and fittingly has as its main theme 'Joint Action for Mission'. It was resolved that instead of waiting for organic Church unity churches should do together now what can best be done by the pooling of their resources. While the majority of the evangelical and interdenominational societies could not approve the integration of the IMC into the WCC, there has been evidence during the past twenty years of a new spirit of working together which augurs well for the Seventies.

In Africa and Asia there are a number of national Evangelical Fellowships, many of which are associated with the World Evangelical Fellowship, which was formed in 1951. Through them evangelical Christians from all over each country come together in concerted study, prayer and action. Typical and exemplary among them is the Evangelical Fellowship of India. This has been active in a number of ways. It has conducted Conferences, Pastors' Retreats, Evangelistic Campaigns, and finally has organized its own Missionary Society. Along the way it brought into being the Evangelical Literature Fellowship of India, co-ordinating the work of the evangelical publishers and presses; the Evangelical Radio Fellowship of India, an attempt to bring together radio programmers throughout the country, and also the Christian Education Evangelical Fellowship of India, producing graded Sunday School lessons over wide linguistic areas of the country. It brought together all evangelicals on the basis of a common acceptance of a statement of faith and debarred none of them on the grounds of their other allegiances. The EFI grows in its significance. For those churches with no global association, it may well form the basis of continuing fellowship and help for missionaries from overseas, for as long as they may continue to enter, it could form the advisory base. The Commission agrees with the 1966 Wheaton Congress on this issue: 'We will encourage and assist in the organization of evangelical fellowships among churches and missionary societies at national, regional, and international levels.' It must be recognized, however, that there should be no attempt to manipulate these fellowships as the instruments of missionary society interests to the disadvantage of national churches, or to use them as structures for the maintaining of colonial-style controls over national churches.

In recent years, there have been two outstanding examples of partnership overseas with regard to two countries long closed to the traditional missionary outreach. These examples certainly could be called patterns for the future, although the second is likely to be a more permanent pattern than the first.

In 1954 opportunity was given to start Christian work in Nepal, a country that by tradition was hyper-conservative in its Hinduism, and in spite of fifteen years of contact with a torrent of outside influences—social, industrial, cultural and religious—still is conservative. Four or five societies had been waiting for a long time to start work there, and when the Government gave as their condition the starting of medical work on a large scale it was realized to be impracticable for the available personnel in any one Society. So the United Mission to Nepal was brought into being, and through the sixteen years of its existence has grown to include some twenty-eight member churches and missions. It represents almost all Protestant denominations—Lutherans, Methodist, Anglican, Presbyterian, Mennonite, etc.—while its personnel are drawn from twelve countries, East and West. It is not the only Mission in Nepal (there are two or three others) but with its 130 workers it is engaged in medical and educational work, assisting and encouraging the tiny church in Nepal.

The other concerns Afghanistan. This is not a United Mission in the precise terms of the United Mission to Nepal. The UMN is organized as a mission with its headquarters in Kathmandu, but the Afghanistan venture is the grouping of medical teams under direct contract to government with any overall 'mission' control very much in the background. The priority is, and must be, the medical task in which they are engaged—there is no church in the land, but these Christian workers are in daily contact with people. This may well be a pattern to be followed—not closely organized mission, but fellowships of believers engaged in professional pursuits, known and sought after for their skills but still witnesses through whom the Spirit of God may work.

Reference has already been made to the partnership of missionary societies with existing churches, and one remarks that the degree of mobility and flexibility that such societies are able to achieve stamps it as an enduring pattern for today. Besides the valuable pastoral ministry that such missions can afford to churches, and the specialized help and initiative they are giving in the realms of Christian literature, writing, production and distribution, and in radio, there are two areas of partnership that we note for special mention. Both, in a sense, have been pioneered in Latin America, but the second particularly comes at a time of deeper concern and awareness in other parts of the world.

Evangelism

In the past two years, Congresses on Evangelism have been held in strategic centres in West Africa, Singapore, and Colombia, drawing representatives of churches and missions from all over Africa, Asia, and Latin America. From each there emerged a profound sense of national responsibility for the evangelization of their continents. Churches and individuals have moved away from narrow parochial concern to think of whole countries and continents. This change has come about, of course, by the revolution in communication, in the sense both of transportation and the use of the mass media, but in no small degree is due to the experiments in nation-wide evangelism that have been so successfully carried out, first in Latin America and now more specifically in sub-Saharan Africa. There can be no escaping the fact that the 'saturation evangelism' movements on both continents have been inspired and sponsored largely by missionaries from outside, but such has been their planning and operation that they have been able to involve the churches in a way unprecedented in the history of modern missions.

'Evangelism-in-Depth' in Latin America is very ably described by one of its exponents, W. Dayton Roberts, in *Revolution in Evangelism* (Scripture Union). Kenneth Strachan's basic theory was, 'The growth of any movement is in direct proportion to the success of that movement in mobilizing its total membership in the constant propagation of its beliefs', and through the years from the first Evangelism-in-Depth campaign which took place during 1960 in Nicaragua right through to that in Colombia in 1968, missionaries from outside and local church leaders worked together to make each succeeding campaign more the work of the total Protestant community in the particular country concerned. The results were quite dramatic. In Bolivia in 1965, for instance, it is estimated that 18,000 Christians participated in the visitation programme, and that during the year there were about 20,000 professions of faith. The training programmes, the insistence on the vital place of prayer-cells (there were 4,204 of these in Bolivia), were not just for the year but have played their part in a continuing urge to evangelize in the churches. Surely there can be no greater pattern of partnership than the total mobilization of the Christian community, the pooling of all resources in men and money to accomplish a goal of national evangelization.

The movement spreads. It has its centre for Asia in Indonesia, again headed by a 'foreign missionary' but one who through the strategic thinking of his society has already spent many years in the local churches stimulating personal evangelism.

It is in Africa, however, that it is really playing an important rôle in the patterns of Church growth that dominate the life of the Protestant Churches in this post-colonial period. 'New Life for All', commenced in Nigeria, and again spearheaded by missionaries, has become the method of the churches in reaching their neighbours. This is, for Africa, a continuing programme of evangelism. It is reported that since its inception in 1964 in Northern Nigeria there has been an average annual church growth rate there of 39 per cent. So successful has it been in Nigeria that at the time of the Commission there are saturation evangelism programmes operating or being planned in twenty-seven of the thirty-four sub-Saharan countries of Africa.

Theological Education

A recent Indian writer in the ecumenical journal *International Review of Missions* (October, 1970) with his subject 'Racist Assumptions of the 19th Century Missionary Movement', said, 'There is a particular need to examine the evangelical theology of the 19th century and of some circles even now, to see if it does not arise directly from racist assumptions and lead to racist practices'. Whatever such an examination may reveal, we would probably agree with what Bruce Nicholls has said in his article 'Towards an Asian Theology of Mission' (*Evangelical Missions Quarterly:* Winter 1970): viz. 'The problem of western missions is to accept the disaccommodation of their western structure in order to allow national churches to develop their own forms. The evident failure of the missionary movement to do this is perhaps one indication of our lack of trust in the Holy Spirit to illuminate the truth revealed and communicated in Scripture to the mind and lives of Asian believers'. Therefore we can welcome two important developments in theological education in which missionaries from overseas and the churches overseas themselves are engaged. The preparation of adequate evangelical leadership for the churches overseas must take an increasing slice of the 'missionary cake' in terms of personnel and budget. Reference has already been made to consideration being given by EMA societies jointly towards better staffing and upgrading of existing Bible Colleges and Theological Seminaries, and it is obvious that this is basically necessary and would in turn both help and be helped by the two developments now being described.

(*a*) Theological Commissions

There is, all too tardily, a recognition that adequate theological preparation for the ministry in a given country and society with its own cultural and religious background must be carried out with adequate understanding of these social and cultural factors. A number of Evangelical Fellowships have set up Theological Commissions to study particularly the theological implications for the presentation of the Gospel within the prevailing culture. This kind of commission must be seen as entirely separate from the universalistic approach which would suggest, for instance, that devout Hindus, by reason of their sincerity, and the good works which they do under the inspiration of their faith, are really covered by the atoning work of Christ, and need only to be awakened to a knowledge of that work.

Evangelical theologians from all over Asia are busy working together towards an Asian confession of the Gospel, relevant to the issues of the contemporary Asian revolution, and at the same time subordinate and subject to Scripture. Similar efforts are being made in Latin America, and missionaries of long experience in these lands are making a real contribution by their encouragement of national theologians. Those interested in this particular development should take *Theological News*, published by the Theological Assistance Programme of the World Evangelical Fellowship (obtainable through the Evangelical Alliance). It will be seen that development in this direction will affect not only the curricula of the Bible and Theological Colleges, but also their structure.

(*b*) Theological Education by Extension

A growing church situation in Latin America revealed that the current residential Bible Institute method was not only inadequate to train leaders in sufficient numbers, but also was often far from ideally suited to training men and women to work in the local church situations.

An experiment which was commenced in Guatemala in 1963 for the 200 Presbyterian congregations has been developed in Colombia,

Brazil, and Bolivia and is seen as a major breakthrough in theological education for the thousands of church leaders. This system, known as Theological Education by Extension, takes the tutor out to centres within a 60-mile radius where he meets his students in their local church and social environment at any one of five academic levels to which the students may attain. This has brought many more students into regular and systematic theological training than was possible in the residential institute. It enables mature Christian leaders and workers to receive this education whereas it is usually only the young and relatively immature that could leave their homes to come into residence for a long period of time. The main disadvantage is the time taken to complete a course, and only if a student could study five hours each day at home, and five hours each week with his visiting tutor, could he complete this course in the three years taken by a residential student. Thus, according to time he can give, the extension student could take anything from three to fifteen years; but the two main advantages are, first that he is studying at his own intellectual and local church level, where his ministry is being exercised; and secondly, a long weekly contact with his tutor should benefit him greatly in the subjective part of his studies.

But if this is to be successful and fulfil the high hopes entertained, it is going to involve partnership with missionaries from overseas as well as national leaders to provide, first, the programmed lessons, a far more demanding and costly exercise than the writing of traditional text books for classroom lectures; and then for the adequate staffing of the teaching centres from which the tutors go out weekly to many groups. In a survey by the EMA two years ago it was estimated that only 5 per cent of the total missionary strength was engaged in Bible School work. If this Theological Education by Extension is to prove successful then we estimate that at least 15 per cent of missionary strength should be devoted to it as first priority.

There is one area of partnership which deserves a section to itself because of its increasing importance in these days. Not only are the opportunities for the traditional 'full-time' missionary entrance being restricted in certain countries, but also there is a new emphasis throughout the church all over the world upon lay witness. The non-professional missionary has always had an important part to play in the overall missionary outreach of the church.

8. The Non-Professional Missionary

Although the growing importance of the laity is becoming generally recognized in the church in this country, the image of overseas mission that our churches cling to is that of the full-time missionary *called* and *committed* for life to a missionary society, and preferably working in a primitive area. The Christian public is less ready to realize that the teacher in a large secondary school in Africa, the engineer in Malaysia, the administrator in the service of an independent Government, or the VSO working for a couple of years on a literacy project in India, may regard himself as much a missionary as those described in the previous sentence. All are motivated by the Holy Spirit and sent to a specific task, and all can fulfil a vital rôle in helping establish a live church in a developing country.

Such partners are not new in missionary strategy. The Roman soldiers, administrators and merchants who took the gospel to the boundaries of the Roman Empire; indeed, some of the pioneers of the great evangelical missionary movement of the 18th and 19th centuries, originally went overseas under non-mission auspices. William Carey established himself as a printer and teacher in Serampore, because at first he lacked formal denominational sponsorship, and David Livingstone's second journey of exploration up the Zambezi River was made under the joint sponsorship of the British Government and the Royal Geographical Society. But perhaps the last twenty years (the period immediately following the granting of political independence to former British colonies) has seen the greatest need for various forms of professional and technical assistance in countries determined to reach the point of 'economic take-off' as quickly as possible and thus be less dependent on foreign aid. Pressing needs have been felt in the fields of education, engineering, medicine, and finance. Although some missionary societies have already established first-class secondary schools within their areas of influence, independent Governments are reluctant to continue to encourage an educational policy that is avowedly denominational and mission-controlled, and have themselves assumed the major responsibility for recruiting staff and declaring policy for universities, schools and hospitals. There is an urgent need for medical staff for the new hospitals (often built with foreign aid), and in some countries there are still insufficient local skilled engineering personnel to build roads and dams, or to introduce new technical processes to modernize an economic structure often twenty of more years out of date.

The young Christian graduates of the Fifties and Sixties saw these opportunities as strategic and exciting, and a steady flow of men and women with professional skills, but above all a sense of missionary vocation, have been filling these posts. Methods of recruitment vary. The Ministry of Overseas Development is probably the largest official organization in the recruiting field. It recruits teachers and lecturers, engineers and other technical experts appointed to the countries in receipt of British aid. Today there are about 15,000 personnel overseas working in one or other of these capacities, and sponsored by the British aid programme.

Various agencies

Usually the government that employs these technical experts pays their basic salaries, and the Ministry adds an expatriate allowance, together with a gratuity at the end of the contract (pensionable terms are very rarely offered by governments nowadays). Some governments prefer to recruit personnel direct, and a number have London offices with this responsibility. University posts overseas are either advertised by the University direct, or through the Inter-University Council, a kind of academic clearing house for posts of this sort. Business organizations in need of overseas personnel (banks, oil companies, mining concerns, etc.) also recruit directly through their London offices.

Certain Christian organizations quickly realized that they would do well to advertise and promote this kind of appointment, and the IVF Graduates' Fellowship and the Overseas Appointments Bureau, two of the bodies in touch with Christian professional people, regularly advertise posts abroad.

Voluntary Service Overseas also offers an opportunity for younger people to serve overseas in less executive positions but with service and adventure as the driving motives. VSO was formed in 1958 largely in answer to a letter written to the *Sunday Times* by the present Bishop of Norwich, pointing out that the end of National Service offered a pool of talented young people that could well be used to help provide desperately needed skills in developing countries. The letter ended thus:—

'It will be necessary for somebody—or bodies—to accept responsibility for three things: for selecting suitable boys and suitable projects, for finding travelling expenses, and for ensuring that at the other end there is someone who will meet the boys and set them on the right road. Is it beyond our organisational capacity to unite these needs?'

VSO was the answer, and in 1968/69 was responsible for sending over 1,000 qualified volunteers—and not only 'boys', as the worthy Bishop envisaged—into 60 countries. They perform a variety of jobs.

Although VSO is not a religious organization, it has close links with Christian Aid, and about 200 volunteers annually work in Christian Aid projects, part of their costs being met by Christian Aid.

So far this survey has been concerned with men and women working in entirely secular capacities, and whose explicit Christian witness is limited to their unofficial activities. This statement itself can be very misleading, because a Christian teacher or engineer in a developing country who approaches his job with integrity, determined to work to the best of his ability, anxious to understand the problems of the country and not concerned just with making a lot of money and isolating himself from the local people *is* making a vital contribution to missionary enterprise.

Yet there is another group to be considered; those who work on a short-time contractual basis within a missionary society. Although the general policy of missionary bodies is to ask for life commitment, a few are beginning to appreciate the value of a limited number of *short-term* workers, appointed for specific positions. The SUM, for example, appoints Christian graduates to teach in their educational establishments in Nigeria for periods of one year upwards; the OMF recently announced its willingness to accept short-term workers for certain specific positions; some have already been appointed on this basis. The OMF also agrees to second a few full members (recruited under normal conditions) with particular teaching or medical skills to specific institutions. One is lecturing in Surgery at the University of Chiengmai and another in Advanced Physics in the University of North Sumatra. The Methodist Missionary Society makes careful efforts to find appointments for short-term professional Christian people from its own denomination, either through the Overseas Appointments Bureau, or, in some cases direct from a school or hospital that has close links with Methodism. Furthermore, and just as important, the MMS gets in contact with the Methodist Church nearest to the town to which the worker is going, and 'membership rights' are mutually transferable. Sometimes, too, young Methodists who go overseas with VSO are linked with Methodist institutions.

Opportunities for Christian Service

What opportunities for involvement in local Christian activity does the non-professional missionary find? The answer will vary from one setting to another, but in areas where English is the lingua franca opportunities can be considerable. For example, Scripture Union activities in Ghana have grown from modest beginnings in 1952, when a small group of teachers and lecturers organized the first Inter-College Camp, to a flourishing locally sponsored and financed set-up, with three full-time staff workers and an average of seven camps each year, together with training schools, two vacation Bible Schools for children, and a Sixth Form Vacation Course (similar to those organized by the Inter-School Christian Fellowship in Britain). The bulk of the organization came from the 'non-professional missionaries'—teachers, lecturers, architects, nurses and others—who have given their time and energy on a completely voluntary basis.

Nor is this kind of influence confined to the menfolk. The wife of a UNESCO specialist attached to the University College of Dar-es-Salaam has for some years been an Editorial Secretary of the Africa Christian Press. She encourages Africans to write scripts on topics of concern for the young Christian in an African setting, helps them (sometimes by re-writing their scripts for them) and has produced a book *Adventure with a Pen* giving practical advice to potential writers. In thinking of the role of expatriate women in Africa today, nobody could dare begin to evaluate the effect of a thousand Christian open homes that welcome the student or the nurse for an evening's relaxed fellowship.

Similar opportunities for work among young people at school and college exist in most of the countries of independent Africa. Other avenues of service include running Sunday Schools, involving oneself in the local church (although this will sometimes mean the 'expatriates' church), helping with Scout and Guide organizations, and in some cases sharing in the fellowship of the national Church.

In many ways this type of 'non-professional' missionary is ideally suited to this particular kind of service. They *know* the young people whom they hope to meet and work with at camp or vacation school, they have generous holidays, and are able to devote time to this kind of activity—and they have the respect of the young intelligentsia of the country. Unfortunately, the fact that most of the missionaries have established their work in the up-country (and therefore more backward) areas has associated the concepts of 'primitiveness' and 'simple-minded natives' with the missionaries. This concept may well be mistaken and sometimes unkind, but nevertheless persists in the thinking of the rather arrogant intelligentsia. Fortunately some of the more recent SU camps in Ghana, for example, have been staffed by Ghanaians and expatriates together, by 'non-professional' and 'professional' missionaries—an excellent arrangement.

It should perhaps be pointed out that the relationship between missionaries (in the traditional sense) and those working in a secular capacity has not always been altogether happy. There are reasons on both sides; the missionary may well regard the young teacher or engineer as out to make money, and may find it difficult not to envy his higher standard of living. Then he may regard his stay as so brief as to be of little permanent value to the Church; after all, the missionary sowed the seed faithfully for five years or more before he was privileged to see any results, and the non-professionals often do not stay as long as that. Another misconception that has grown up has been for the more educated national Christians to associate themselves more easily with the non-professional Christian groups (College CU's, etc.) and thus leave the less well qualified to help the mission stations.

Some Recommendations

All these dangers must be realized; but nevertheless this Commission accepts that the rôle played by the non-professional missionary in helping to establish and strengthen the Church overseas is vital, and whole-heartedly recommends this form of service to those with certain professional skills to offer. We also recommend that more care be taken: (a) To link up Christian personnel going overseas with missionaries, but more particularly with the local church, in order to help them to enjoy fellowship when they arrive. This seems to be particularly necessary for VSO's going overseas for a year or two. (b) To encourage more careful—and planned—integration between short-term workers and long-term missionaries in the overseas Church. Short-term personnel should be given as much background information as possible about the area in which they are working and their skills used in the local Church in the most practicable way. (c) To ensure that non-professional personnel make more effort to have enough knowledge of the local language to enable them to be useful in the local Church. A non-Swahili-speaker in East Africa would be unable to identify himself with the people to whom he has gone to witness. VSO offer a crash course in Swahili to volunteers going to East Africa, and the School of Oriental and African Studies in London regularly runs seminars in a number of languages widely spoken in Africa and Asia. Perhaps Wycliffe Bible Translators would be interested in organizing short courses on a similar basis.

Personnel proceeding overseas usually receive some formal briefing relevant to the appointment they are taking up. Many commercial firms and the Ministry of Overseas Development often send personnel to the excellent briefing courses organized by the Overseas Service College at Farnham Castle.

(d) The Commission would like to see more care taken in providing adequate briefing for Christians about to take up secular appointments overseas. This might take the form of a Christian centre of information about opportunities abroad, and also up-to-date

105

information regarding the position of missions in areas where any concentration of expatriate personnel might be expected. Robin Crawford, Director of 'Christian Preparation for Work Abroad', set up by CBMS, is trying to do just this by means of weekend residential courses and by arranging for personnel going overseas for the first time to meet others with several years' experience. The Inter-Varsity Fellowship has been doing a similar job in a small way for many years through its annual Overseas Service Conference in July.

Missionary training colleges should be encouraged to offer short briefing courses for those going overseas in a secular capacity. Some already do: All Nations Christian College is one such. More courses are urgently needed of a different nature from the longer and more theologically biased courses for 'professional' missionaries, but offering valuable information about the religious (Christian and otherwise) background of various regions; perhaps missionaries and church leaders overseas could offer 'Instruction Weeks' to non-professional missionaries which would provide an opportunity both to meet Christians and also to answer questions that have arisen concerning the areas in which they are working.

Often a couple of years' experience in another country will make a more detailed refresher course much more meaningful, and Christians in professional posts overseas could well be encouraged to attend such courses during their first leave.

(e) Another present weakness concerns the attitude of the 'home' churches to the 'non-professional missionary'. Although missionaries working for a society are usually given a valedictory service, and prayer links are maintained throughout the period overseas, at present this happens less frequently for teachers and other technical advisers.

The home churches of such 'Christian workers overseas' should regard them in the same context as their traditional missionaries, assuring them of prayer support and doing all possible to maintain contact with them when they are overseas. Where possible, the home church should also contact the missionary society (denominational or not, according to the local context and the interest of the church) in the area to which the worker was going.

Finally, and perhaps most important, we need to destroy the mistaken idea that 'non-professional' and 'professional' missionaries have different motives in serving overseas. Missionary societies need to recognize the strategic importance of this new 'battalion', while the Christian in secular service overseas need to understand more fully the task of the professional missionary, and look to him for fellowship and guidance regarding the best way in which he can serve the Master. The key word should be *Partnership*—working together for Christ.

Chapter 5

Future Patterns of Partnership

1. Is Partnership needed?

As earlier chapters have shown, the Christian Church is now in existence in nearly every country of the world. Since people can be reached most easily and most effectively with the gospel by people of their own colour and culture, some might think that we should now leave the Church in each country to get on with the job of evangelism among its own people, and not confuse the issue by trying to bring help from abroad.

With the decline in Christianity in Western Europe this argument has special appeal here. Why send missionaries to Africa where the Church is growing fast and is on the whole quite capable of looking after itself when there is so much work to be done in Britain?

There are six reasons at least why we should still be deeply involved in the spread of the gospel round the world.[1]

First, because Christ's command still stands: 'Go, then to all peoples everywhere and make them disciples.' Moreover, someone has pointed out that it is written in virtually every language into which Scriptures have been translated. 'All peoples everywhere' have the duty to go and tell the good news as well as the right to hear.

Second, because there are still many countries of the world where Christians are only a tiny fraction of the population. In Thailand, for example, there is a church in being: just over 30,000 Protestant Christians, according to the statistics. But there are 35 million people there who do not know Christ, and it is our responsibility, along with the Thai Christians, to see that the present generation there hears about Him.

Equally, of course, it is the duty of Thai Christians, in so far as their small numbers allow, to go to all peoples everywhere. No doubt most of their efforts will be directed towards their own people. But as opportunities come to reach others they are taking them. Four Thai Christians, for example, have recently gone to Laos to

107

help with the medical work of the Asian Christian Service Unit. It should not surprise us to find countries that used to be thought of as 'receiving' countries in the missionary enterprise becoming 'sending' countries as well. So in 1968 Mitsuru Iwai arrived in Indonesia from Japan as a missionary with Scripture Union—one of a small but increasing number of Asians working as full-time missionaries in other countries.

Britain is beginning to receive help from countries to whom she has for many years sent missionaries, particularly from overseas students. For example, a few years ago a group of Nigerians started the Christian Union at St. David's College, Lampeter, in Wales. The Christian Unions at a number of other colleges in Britain, such as the Holborn College of Law, were started by other overseas students, and more established Christian Unions have called on them to take leadership responsibility. A Christian student from Ghana, for example, took over as President at Birmingham University when the native British students were sadly divided, and his tact and balance pulled the Christian Union together.

Third, we should give substantial help to work in the developing countries just because the churches are growing so fast in many of them, as we have seen in earlier chapters. Some people argue the other way, and say that because people are so unresponsive in Britain we should concentrate our efforts here. But in many parts of the world today the Holy Spirit has prepared people for the message in a wonderful way. There are non-Christians who really want to know about Christ and to start to follow Him: and thousands of young believers who want to know more. If we could see the whole picture, as God sees it, and really cared for all men equally, it would surely be to these where God is so evidently at work that we would make sure to go. Love would compel us to do so. And so would considerations of strategy. As Dr. D. A. McGavran has put it: if 'concentration of resources on growing points comes to be the strategy of missions, we shall find ourselves in a new era of advance'. [2]

Fourth, even in countries with a high proportion of Christians, many church leaders are asking for help. One of the staff of the Christian Council in Ghana (a country in which 43 per cent registered as Christians in the 1960 census) recently drew up a list of areas where help was urgently needed from abroad: literature, broadcasting, theological education, pastors' conferences, correspondence courses, and evangelism among Muslims were some of the priorities. The wealth of experience of the worldwide Church in these special fields could help the Ghana Church tremendously.

While working on this Report, the Commission sent a questionnaire to a number of Christian leaders in different countries asking what help churches in Britain could give churches in the developing countries in the next decade. One question was 'Will churches in your country need help from overseas in the next ten years?' Nearly everyone thought they would. Dr. B. Chew, for example, from Singapore, writes: 'Definitely, yes. Singapore cannot exist economically without outside co-operative help. Spiritually, growth and mission would dwindle without a supraracial and supranational outlook and outside help.' Mr. Theodore Williams, an Indian from Bangalore, writes: 'Highly qualified people who would train the nationals are needed. These must come to work not in the spirit of an expert, but in the spirit of a partner.'

Mission leaders consulted felt the same. Bishop A. C. Stanway, from Dodoma, Tanaznia writes: 'All well-developed countries realize that progress in under-developed countries will be too slow unless there is stimulation from without. They would not want help to keep growing or to grow, but they would want it if they are to grow faster than the population.' Michael Griffiths of the OMF says this: 'We anticipate that the population in the area in which we are working, at present 372 million people in countries open to the gospel, will increase by 1980 to approximately 478 millions. We face an increase of about 106 million people. To those of us who live here and have the opportunity of travelling widely throughout the area, it is clear that the national churches, which even now are scarcely making much of an impact in most countries upon the unreached multitudes, are even less likely to be able to have an effective outreach on all these new people when the population is increasing so fast, without help from the international Church.'

On the other hand, Mr. Chua Wee Hian from Singapore writes: 'Frankly, no, if financial help is meant, as our country is economically well off and Christians are mainly in the middle class bracket. But if specialized personnel help is offered, yes.' In answering the question 'What would happen if no help from overseas were given?' no one felt that Christian witness would come to an end. 'Activities would still go on, but on a much reduced scale', writes Dr. Williams. 'In the long run the local church would gradually recover and learn to be self-dependent, and embark on only those schemes which could be financed locally,' says the Rev. David Gitari, from Kenya.

Although they believe the church could survive on its own, and although in some countries there are difficulties caused by political or nationalistic factors, most Christian leaders round the world are saying firmly 'Come over and help us.' It would be tragic if this appeal were to be ignored.

The *fifth* reason why Christians in the West should be concerned about and involved in the life of the churches in the developing countries is that we are all bound together in the body of Christ. Paul is writing of the worldwide Church when he says: 'He appointed some to be apostles, others to be prophets, others to be evangelists, others to be pastors and teachers. He did this to prepare all God's people for the work of Christian service, to build up the body of Christ. . . . Under His control all the different parts of the body fit together, and the whole body is held together by every joint with which it is provided. So when each separate part works as it should, the whole body grows and builds itself up through love.' (Ephesians 4.11,12,16. Today's English Version.) Each part of the body has its own contribution to make to the evangelism of the world and the building up of the Church. As Mr. P. T. Chandapilla writes from Madras, 'All churches in all nations need help from one another.'

This, of course, is quite different from the idea to which many have become accustomed, in which Europe and North America give all the help, and Africa, Latin America, and Asia receive it. A Christian in Holland who saw the EA questionnaire complained that it was out of date to ask such things. 'Last year I travelled through Indonesia and visited the fastest-growing churches of the world. You know, I became a bit jealous. I feel they could teach us a lot—if only what commitment means. Perhaps our questionnaire should not ask "How can we help?" but "How can we be helped?"'

This leads on to the *sixth* reason for involvement. If Christians in the West think only about their own problems, and forget about their responsibilities round the world, they will miss a great deal. Bishop Stanway writes: 'The church that doesn't want to look outside its own country will probably die anyway. You just can't live unto yourself.'

Western churches have vast assets which should be made available to the Church worldwide: assets of money certainly, though, as we have seen, some areas overseas do not need that particular form of help; but, more important, a wealth of Christian experience, built up over centuries; vast assets of trained men and women whose help is desperately needed round the world.

If we fail to share these assets, the worldwide Church will suffer loss, but we ourselves will be even more impoverished. There is tremendous zeal and enthusiasm in many churches in Africa, Asia, and Latin America that put older and sleepier churches to shame. Writing in the *Church of England Newspaper*, 8th May, 1970, Michael Fleming described what is happening in Northern Nigeria, for example. In the two provinces of Zaria and Plateau '7,000 groups met daily to pray. In one village, with a population of 1,000, fourteen prayer cells were established, and in a town of 10,000, no fewer than 117 groups gathered each day for prayer.' Small wonder that 'Church membership has increased by an annual average of 35 per cent. Attendance in 1965 in Northern Nigeria was approximately 284,000 but only three years later this had mushroomed to 480,000.' There must be few Western Christians who have had the privilege of seeing what God is doing in areas like this who have not been humbled, challenged, and inspired by the experience.

We conclude this section with *one example of how partnership can work*. In January 1964 a dozen men and women met in a small room in Christiansborg, a suburb of Accra, in Ghana, to discuss how to produce Christian literature that would be on the right wavelength for young people in that country. There was a sense of urgency about the meeting, as one of the people who should have been present had just been arrested, suspected of political agitation. Most of those there were involved in Christian work among the more educated section of Ghana's rising generation, helping school Scripture Union groups and camps, advising the university Christian Union, leading Bible classes in the city, and so on. All had found that, provided it was not too expensive, young people were keen to buy Christian literature in English. The problem was that most of what was available was written originally for Britain or America, and was not really suitable. *Towards Christian Marriage* (IVP), for example, was selling in good numbers, but the cultural patterns are so different that it wasn't really answering many of the young people's problems. So Africa Christian Press was born.

The group in Accra recognized straightaway that it needed to think internationally. Already some of those present had been in correspondence with other parts of Africa and with Christians in London. It was decided to publish for the whole of English-speaking Africa. Experience has since shown that there is sufficient similarity of culture across the Continent for this to be possible. So people were invited from other parts of the Continent to be corresponding members of the Committee. Because of slow communications within Africa it was decided to print and store books in England, and the Inter-Varsity Press agreed to look after that side of things. No one in the Accra group had much experience of publishing, so IVP's knowledge was a tremendous help. Substantial capital was needed, since printers have to be paid before the books can be sold; here again Christians in Britain were able to help, and without them the project would probably never have got off the ground. The search for an artist who could convincingly draw African faces led to Australia. When the books were produced, it was found that there was quite a demand for them in India and New Guinea, as well as all over Africa. Prayer partners were enlisted in many countries round the world. Five years later a third of a million books had been sold. Most of the writers were Africans. So were most of the readers. But the assistance of the world Church, artistic skill from Australia, and publishing know-how and money from England and prayer from around the world made it possible for one to speak to the other.

More and more it is being recognized today that the world is one. In the development of its economic resources, in the control of pollution, in combating disease, no nation can afford to stand on its own. If churches round the world are going to grapple with the problems of the 70's, keep up with exploding populations, and obey our Lord's command to go to all men everywhere with the message of hope, they must stand and work and pray together.

2. Will Partnership be Possible?

Once we have decided that different sections of the church have a continuing responsibility to help one another, we come up against the problem of 'No Entry' signs. In 1961 all foreign missionaries had to leave China. In 1966 they were turned out of Burma. Since 1967 Malaysia has ruled that no foreign missionary might stay for more than ten years in the country, on the grounds that by that time a national should be ready to take over his work. Since 1964 missionaries have been kept out of the South of the Sudan, though recently the government has agreed to change the rule so that it only affects missionaries who are not Africans. It is increasingly difficult to get permission for new missionaries to work in India; and those already in the country have to re-apply for a resident's permit each year. Many people feel that the doors for missionary opportunity are closing so rapidly that though we wish to work with out brethren round the world, we may not be able to do so much longer.

Most of the 'No Entry' signs are there for political rather than anti-Christian reasons. Apparently they have not always hindered the growth of the Church. 'Since the missionaries were expelled from the Southern Sudan, the Church there has continued to grow at a phenomonal rate despite the destruction of its institutions and the scattering of its people.' J. V. Taylor in *CMS Newsletter*, July 1968. Encouraging news continues to come from Burma, where the churches are pressing on in evangelism and the necessary network of service agencies is being developed.

These signs should be a warning to all of us to prepare churches in every country for the withdrawal of foreign help, in men and money, in case that day should come. They should also encourage us to look for other kinds of co-operation. Some countries closed to those labelled as 'missionaries' will welcome business men and teachers from abroad, including Christians if they come to do a good job of work (see ch. 4). Such men and women can have fellowship with the local church and be a great strength and encouragement to it. Other countries which will not accept resident missionaries will welcome short-term visitors. Speakers can be supplied for conferences, short theological lecture tours arranged, and other specialist help given. Although selection needs to be made with great care, the money formerly used for paying missionaries can be diverted for training national Christian leaders, where necessary in other countries. Students from the 'closed' countries can be met and befriended in the great universities of the world.

Moreover, while a few doors have closed, new ones have opened. For example, in 1970 the Red Sea Mission Team was invited to send doctors, nurses and teachers into the Yemen, a country where Christian work had never before been permitted. Today there are many more doors open than there are missionaries available to walk through them; and the uncertainty as to how long some of them will remain open merely underlines the urgency of buying up present opportunities. 'We must work . . . while it is day; night comes, when no one can work.' (John 9.4, RSV.)

3. What kind of help will be most useful?

The kind of aid needed will obviously vary from place to place, depending on the local situation. Michael Griffiths of the OMF suggests three categories of country:

'Group 1. *Pioneer Phase Countries*, that is to say, countries which are scarcely evangelized, like *Laos*, *Cambodia* and *Thailand*. In Thailand approximately one in every thousand people is a 'professing Christian' of some kind, but it needs to be remembered that these are largely either of an ethnically Chinese background (i.e., not Thai Buddhists), leprosy patients, or to be found in two restricted areas of the country centring on Bangkok and Chiengmai. OMF has approximately 200 missionaries in Thailand, but many of these are engaged in reaching ethnic minorities, namely the million Muslims (of Malay background) in the south, and the tribal groups on the northern borders. . . . Thailand needs more Christians from the international Church to help it in this pioneer stage. These of course are not all westerners, and we already have Filipinos and Chinese working with us and we anticipate more Chinese if possible, although they have far greater visa problems than do Westerners.'

In areas like this the need is clearly for pioneer evangelists, men and women who will get to know the languages and the cultures really well over a number of years, and make Christ known through life and lip so that churches will be planted. Some of them must be gifted in evangelism, some in preaching, some in personal work, some in giving pastoral help to those who come to believe. Medical workers, Bible translators, literature specialists, experts in radio and television will all be needed. For the local church, even if it exists, has as yet few resources of its own. Mr. Griffiths goes on to speak of:

'Group II. *Patch-work Phase Countries.* There are existing national churches in *Malaysia*, for example, but their strength is to be found among the English-educated Chinese immigrants. There are some fine older Chinese language churches but by and large there has been little Christian impact upon the poorer, dialect-speaking Chinese or on the Tamils on the plantations, and of course among Malays Christian preaching is entirely forbidden. Here then you have a social patch-work. Vast areas racially and socially are almost without any Christian penetration at all. We are now seeing the beginnings of a stirring among the English-educated group in seeing responsibility for the poorer masses. In *Japan*, with at most one per cent of the population nominally Christian, these are mainly city people, and the country areas and small towns are still unreached as they were fifty years ago. The city Churches seem to have little sense of concern to reach them. Many Japanese leaders think that while Japanese make better pastors, 'outsiders' often make better pioneer evangelists. The majority of Japanese churches would still seem to be pioneered and begun by foreigners rather than by nationals. Again there are stirrings, but so often the establishment of a local congregation and its perpetuation is thought of as an end in itself. *Indonesia*, although it belongs I believe properly in the third group, also comes here because its 115 million people are really a patch-work of nations and some groups are *not evangelized* at all—for example, the Madurese and Sundanese (both in Java) and the Minangkabau and Achinese (both in Sumatra). Where there has been a patch-work growth rather than a truly nation-wide one, help from the international Church is still necessary in the unevangelized areas.'

In countries in this group, missionaries are needed both in pioneer areas, just as they are in countries in Group I, and also working alongside the national churches, where they exist, as outlined under Group III.

'Group III. *Penetrated Phase Countries. Korea* is the one example in East Asia where a whole country has been properly

114

penetrated and evangelized, but *Indonesia* in certain areas is similar, and in both countries probably more than seven per cent of the total population are professing Christians. While I would agree that "Pioneer church planters" are no longer needed, there is still a need for missionaries of other kinds—for example, for pastoral theology, young people's work, and generally to assist young intellectuals within the churches to face the blasts of secularism. By government order in Indonesia there have to be three hours of "religion" a week taught in all schools. In some areas this means the Bible must be taught. One of our missionaries trains four hundred teachers in such schools. Another is preparing curriculum material for use by such teachers throughout the country.'

If he had been writing about the world as a whole, and not just about South East Asia, Mr. Griffiths would no doubt have mentioned a fourth category of country:

Group IV. *Post-Christian Countries.* Before the rise of Islam, countries like *Turkey* and *Tunisia* had vigorous and flourishing Christian churches. Apart from archaeological remains, hardly a trace of them can be found today. The warning to Ephesus 'I will come to you and remove your lampstand from its place, unless you repent' (Revelation 2.5). has quite literally been fulfilled. Yet our responsibility for 'all peoples everywhere' includes such countries. Somehow ways must be found of reaching them.

Britain and Western Europe might perhaps be put in the same category. The decline has not gone anywhere near as far. But it has certainly begun, and the lesson of history is that it could well continue. To take just one example, in 1969 membership of Baptist churches in Britain decreased by 5,996, or 4.6 per cent, to 274,871 (*Annual Report of the Baptist Union of Great Britain and Ireland*). But it is not only a question of numbers. In another place Michael Griffiths talks about a 'national church which has become devotionally cold, spiritually dead, or theologically apostate. The church has gone into recession and the new generation has still to be evangelized'. (*The Millions*, October 1970, p.95). Many would feel that this is an apt description of churches in Western Europe as they are at present. Perhaps what they need is an infusion of vigorous life from some of the fast-growing churches in other countries where people still expect to see God working.

Training

Most copies of the Commission's questionnaire went to leaders of churches in Groups II and III. In answer to the question 'What sort of help from outside your country will be most valuable?' most put training at the top of the list. 'Personnel who could train Sunday School teachers and evangelical theologians to teach in our seminaries,' answers Mr. Chua Wee Hian from Singapore. 'Preparation of a national ministry to take over *every* kind of responsibility into the hands of the churches: pastors, Biblical teachers, school teachers, etc.' writes Sr. Pedro Arana of Peru.

Training must surely be high on any list of priorities. The aim is that in each area there should be a flourishing indigenous church able to stand on its own feet and play its part in God's total programme of worldwide evangelism. If this is to happen local leadership must develop, and the missionary's prime objective must be to help it to do so. One way is to make sure he gets out of the saddle himself. Another is to teach and train, in all aspects of the task, those who are to be the leaders.

This does not necessarily mean the traditional residential Bible School, Seminary or teacher training college. Christ trained His disciples by apprenticeship, taking them with Him on His travels and setting them to work. The Apostle Paul did the same with Timothy and his colleagues. An important by-product of the evangelistic youth camps run in many parts of the world is the apprentice training given to young Christians who come to help as leaders. Any opportunity for young men and women to be set to work for Christ alongside more experienced colleagues so that they can catch the vision, learn to share their outlook, see how problems can be tackled, should be seen as training of the most practical kind.

Residential colleges have their value, but they are expensive to run. Often the older men who are the natural leaders of the congregations are unable to spare the time for them, and sometimes those who have been to them come back separated by the experience of college from those to whom they are to minister. As we saw in Chapter 4 the idea of the extension seminary has been developed with great success in Latin America to overcome these problems.

A good deal of money has been spent in the last twenty years in sending potential leaders for training overseas. David Gitari, a member of the Commission who has himself benefitted from such training, undertook some research on the effect of such training on those who came to evangelical colleges in Britain between 1960-70. (See pages 92-3). He concludes 'There is no doubt that this training has been a valuable partnership between churches here and overseas, especially during the last six years. This partnership should be continued.' He recommends that greater care should be taken in the selection of candidates, since not all have proved suitable; and that priority should be given to increasing the number of candidates of high intellectual ability who have already had some academic training, to provide the evangelical theologians the younger churches will more and more need in the coming years. He also points out that 'though receiving students here from overseas is an advantage not only to the students but also to the life of the colleges, many more problems could be overcome if there were suitable theological and missionary colleges in the developing countries.'

Of course there are some such colleges but more are needed. And in spite of all that is being done, some churches have hardly any training programme at all. Peter Barker writes about Ghana: 'The Pentecostal and African Independent churches, apart from the Assemblies of God, have no theological college; many of them probably regard such training with suspicion. The team that succeeds in breaking through the suspicion, convincing people concerned of their sincerity and faithfulness to God, and offering a sound Bible training with no denominational strings attached, will do infinite good in churches where there is much zeal and little knowledge.' As we have seen, these churches form the fastest growing section of 'those who profess and call themselves Christians' in Africa, with around seven million adherents.[3] Yet in hardly any of the thirty-four countries where it flourishes is there any formal training available acceptable to its members. What could be done in Africa has been demonstrated in Chile, where the Pentecostal churches contain 80 per cent of Protestants in the country, and the inter-denominational Theological Community runs evening classes in various parts of the country which are greatly valued by the Pente-costal pastors.

But it is not only the leaders who need training. 'If the key to world evangelism is a reproductive witness of the totality of the individual believers, then our first objective had to be *to mobilize and train these Christians* for effective continuous witness in their own countries,' wrote Ken Strachan of the Evangelism-in-Depth Movement. (Quoted by W. Dayton Roberts in *Revolution in Evangelism*, Scripture Union, 1968, p.43.) The application of this principle, of the training of every member of every church, has been a major factor in the rapid church growth in parts of Latin America and Africa through the Evangelism-in-Depth and New Life for All Campaigns.

Young People

'For God's sake do not forget the students and young people,' wrote one, in answer to the Commission's questionnaire. 'Expert missionaries are needed for Sunday School and youth work,' says the Rev. Philip Teng from Hong Kong. 'They should concentrate on student work literature production and technological projects such as radio and mass communications,' answers Mr. P. T. Chandapilla. 'With nearly half the population under fifteen years old and the children's services and Sunday School packed out every Sunday, it is vital to give the teachers more training and to introduce better methods and materials. The opportunity of hundreds of thousands of children in church every week will be lost for ever unless we are more imaginative,' says Peter Barker from Ghana.

Half the population under fifteen—that is quite common in the developing countries. We have seen something of this in Chapter 2. What are the areas where the churches in other countries can help to reach and teach young people?

a. *Children's work*. In African churches, for example, far too often children are treated as they were in Victoria England, as little adults. They have to sit through a long service, trying to keep quiet and as often as not falling off to sleep!

Until he knows the language fluently, someone from abroad cannot do much with younger children direct. The key to the situation is the teachers. In many countries they speak English, though a foreigner will only be able to help them to teach if he has a deep understanding himself of the culture from which the children come.

b. *Secondary Schools*. Not many years ago, in many of the developing countries, churches and missions controlled a good proportion of the available schools. Today while some secondary schools are still under some church influence, nearly all are financed by governments. In the vast majority the most effective Christian work is done through a Christian Union, Scripture Union or other voluntary group, where possible helped by a sympathetic member of staff. Many countries are still eagerly looking for teachers from abroad, and as many have found in recent years the opportunities in such appointments are immense.

c. *Doctors and Nurses*. The devoted work of healing in hundreds of Christian hospitals has effectively shown people that Christ loves them. But often the deepest spiritual response has come from those who train and work in the hospital. Doctors and nurses from abroad can make a major contribution here, and it will be their attitudes of dedication, love and sacrifice that will count just as much as their technical skill. There are also many opportunities in government hospitals, which can lead to the formation of branches of the Nurses' Christian Fellowship, or a

118

similar national movement.

d. *University Students*. In their stirring book *Missions in Crisis* (Inter-Varsity Press, 1961) E. S. Fife and A. F. Glasser urge their readers to concentrate prayer and effort on the student world because it is 'a growing class, a strategic class, a responsive class, a critical class, a needy class, and a neglected class'. Since they wrote these words, the continued increase in student numbers round the world, and the remarkable upturn in student protest and violence have only served to underline their truth. The intervening years have also seen an encouraging increase in Christian witness on the campus; but there are still great opportunities for qualified men and women from abroad who join the staff or work as research students, or take ordinary courses, and by their lives and words strengthen the local team.

One example must suffice. A few years ago a young British mathematician and his family arrived at the Kumasi College of Technology in Ghana. There was no evangelical group on the campus, but after some months they started a weekly Bible study in their home, originally attended by only two students. The group soon became so large that they had to move to a bigger room. Out of it the Christian Fellowship was born, which, within a short time, was being attended by about a third of the students in the College. By 1968 the college had become a university and the Christian Fellowship arranged a mission. Out of 1,500 students, 900 attended the first meeting, an average of 750 attended through the week, and it was estimated that about 1,200 attended at least once. (*PAFES News Bulletin*, April 1969).

There is a key rôle, too, for student organizations equivalent to the IVF. An increasing proportion of their staff are nationals, but not all, and certainly many of them will still need prayer and financial support from other countries for some years.

e. *Youth Groups*. 'If we are to communicate the Christian Faith effectively, we must know and understand the thought forms of our generation. These will differ slightly from place to place, and more so from nation to nation. Nevertheless there are characteristics of an age such as ours which are the same wherever we happen to be' (*Escape from Reason*, by Francis Shaeffer, Inter-Varsity Press, p.7.). The way that Dr. Shaeffer's work at L'Abri has attracted and helped young people from all over the world underlines the point. There is a common youth culture today which is more and more widely accepted by young people who listen to the same music, adopt the same style of dress, demonstrate on the same issues, and have many of the same values and ideals.

As a result, the man who has learned to get on the wave-length of young people in London, Singapore, or New York may be able to get across to young people in Nairobi, Madras, or Paris in a way that an older person from the same country could never do. For young people are facing the same problems, asking the same questions; problems and questions an older generation never thought of. The Youth Fellowship in Kampala, started orginally by a few expatriates, and now run most effectively by a group of young Ugandans, is the sort of project which could be repeated, if there were people to give their time and effort to it, in a thousand cities round the world.

Literature

Millions of boys and girls, whose parents never learned to read, are now at schools, and many adults are taking literacy courses as well. In Ghana for example, school enrolment increased between 1959 and 1966 from 460,000 to 1,130,000 (by nearly 50 per cent in seven years) and the estimate of adult literates by 12 per cent. In Japan literacy is said to be 99 per cent—higher than in Britain.

It is small wonder that church leaders are asking for help in providing reading matter. 'There is no limit to the help needed in this area,' writes Dr. G. D. James from Singapore. At the 1970 Conference of the BMMF in Delhi, mass communications, including literature, were put top of the list of priorities. 'Multiplying millions, who were previously inaccessible, can now hear and read of the love of God. Therefore we need in increasing numbers, on long or short-term contracts, journalists, script writers, drama writers, radio and television personnel, gospel song groups, language specialists, Bible correspondence course teachers and literature agents, retailers, production and promotion specialists.' (*The Telling Times*, BMMF leaflet 1970.)

As far as literature work is concerned, a whole range of skills is needed to take an idea from the mind of the author to that of the reader—or better from potential author to potential reader, since both need training.

The demand for Christian literature in many developing countries is remarkable. Peter Barker, however, sounds a note of caution. 'Literature sold by Christian agencies is usually designed for the British and American markets and is quite unsuitable for Ghana. We have just launched a new five-year project for training writers and producing a new range of books that will be really suitable. Additional skilled help would make a great difference to this project.'

120